European Distance and E-Learning Network Annual Conference (EDEN 2017)

Diversity Matters

Jonkoping, Sweden
13 – 16 June 2017

Editors:

Airina Volungeviciene
Andras Szucs

ISBN: 978-1-5108-5023-1

Printed from e-media with permission by:

Curran Associates, Inc.
57 Morehouse Lane
Red Hook, NY 12571

Printed by Curran Associates, Inc. (2018)

For permission requests, please contact European Distance and E-Learning Network (EDEN)
at the address below.

European Distance and E-Learning Network (EDEN)
Budapest University of Technology & Economics
H-1111 Budapest, Egry J. u.1.
Hungary

Phone: +36 1 463 1628
Fax: +36 1 463 1858

secretariat@eden-online.org

Additional copies of this publication are available from:

Curran Associates, Inc.
57 Morehouse Lane
Red Hook, NY 12571 USA
Phone: 845-758-0400
Fax: 845-758-2633
Email: curran@proceedings.com
Web: www.proceedings.com

EDEN 2017 ANNUAL Conference

Diversity Matters!

EDEN 2017 Annual Conference

Jönköping, Sweden

13-16 June 2017

BOOK OF ABSTRACTS

Including the Collection of "Synergy" Synopses

Edited by

Airina Volungeviciene, András Szűcs
on behalf of the European Distance and E-Learning Network

European Distance and E-Learning Network, 2017

EDEN 2017 Annual Conference
Jönköping, Sweden

Published by the European Distance and E-Learning Network

Editors:

Airina Volungeviciene
András Szűcs

Editorial co-ordination:

Kriszta Mihalyi

EDEN Secretariat, c/o Budapest University of Technology and Economics
H-1111 Budapest, Egry J. u. 1, Hungary
Tel: (36) 1 463 1628, 463 2537
E-mail: secretariat@eden-online.org
http://www.eden-online.org

Conference Publication Sponsor

CONTACT NORTH NORD Online Learning Apprentissage en ligne

Supported by the Erasmus+ Programme of the European Union

Introduction

The skills and knowledge required to take an active part in a society characterised by digital technology are embedded, learned, and practiced in people's daily lives. The ever-changing media- and technology landscapes create opportunities for learning at all stages in life in formal and informal settings. New policies and practices entailed by the high presence of digital tools have to take into account the "inclusion" or "exclusion" of different groups in society.

Technology and open education open doors to groups of learners from a range of backgrounds, generations, cultures with different languages, literacies, and ways of communication. It is difficult in the meantime to meet the evolving skills demand in the globalising value chains. Lifelong Learning is not yet a reality for most!

The behaviour, interests and roles of learners are also repositioned. Technological innovation implies faster learning, and instruction has to be "useful" in order to motivate and engage students. In order to strengthen and stabilise learning, the collaboration between the human mind and the machine have to be regularly reconsidered.

It is of great importance to study **how the educational framing, from policy level down to the actual learning situation, allows for various types of e-learning, open and and distance education**. Diversity also causes fragmentation in learning achievements which should be carefully managed, without loosing identity of learners. One challenge is the often fragmented view of what has been achieved theoretically and practically in this field, and the ever-increasing offer of technology. Co-ordination of information, knowledge and creativity is of high importance for the educational experience.

How do educators deal with diversity in media and technology enhanced learning environments? How can such diversity be accounted for and used to transform and adapt online learning settings? **How do teachers and policy makers meet digital inequalities – what are the impacts of increasing complexity of stakeholder groups of education?** What will be the effects of socio-economic demands and large scale migration on learning?

Will the digital pedagogy arsenal be able to manage diversity in media and technology enhanced learning? How can learning analytics help in assessing and handling diversity in learners background and performance

How do we bring together the strengths of the past with the opportunities for the future?

The responsibility of the scholarly community includes the proper handling of diversity in education with respect to learners' profiles, backgrounds, generations, cultures with different languages, literacies, and ways of communication as well as diversity in media and technology enhanced learning environments. **We need renowned reflections of practice that support paradigm-changing transformations based on systematic knowledge.**

EDEN 2017 is the forum that offers a chance to work together for these goals, and to gain further insight into the core questions.

Ylva Lindberg
Dean of Research, Jönköping University

Airina Volungeviciene
President, EDEN

Acknowledgement and thanks are given to the Programme and Evaluation Committee

Airina Volungeviciene, EDEN President, Vytautas Magnus University, Lithuania
Ylva Lindberg, Jönköping University, Sweden

Diana Andone, Politehnica University of Timisoara, Romania

Deborah Arnold, University of Burgundy, France

Sangeeta Bagga-Gupta, Jönköping University, Sweden

Ulrich Bernath, Ulrich Bernath Foundation for Research in ODL, Germany

Lisa Marie Blaschke, Carl von Ossietzky University of Oldenburg, Germany

Mark Brown, National Institute for Digital Learning, Dublin City University, Ireland

Giulia Messina Dahlberg, Jönköping University, Sweden

Helga Dorner, Central European University, Hungary

Christina Keller, Jönköping University, Sweden

Elsebeth Korsgaard Sorensen, Aalborg University, Denmark

Sandra Kucina Softic, University of Zagreb, Croatia

Fabio Nascimbeni, Universidad Internacional de la Rioja, Spain

Don Olcott Jr., Carl von Ossietzky University of Oldenburg, Germany

Ebba Ossiannilsson, Swedish Association of Distance Education, Sweden

André Petzold, Destination Jönköping, Sweden

Antonella Poce, University Roma III, Italy

Ulf Sandström, Swedish Association for Distance Education, Sweden

Sofoklis Sotiriou, Ellinogermaniki Agogi, Greece

Anette Svensson, Jönköping University, Sweden

Carl-Johan Svensson, Jönköping University, Sweden

Andras Szucs, Secretary General, EDEN, United Kingdom

António Moreira Teixeira, Universidade Aberta, Lisbon, Portugal

Wim Van Petegem, Katholieke Universiteit Leuven, Belgium

Lennart Wass, Jönköping University, Sweden

Steve Wheeler, Chair of EDEN NAP Steering Committee, University of Plymouth, United Kingdom

Madelene Zetterlind, Jönköping University, Sweden

TABLE OF CONTENTS

DIVERSITY AND ICT ENHANCED EDUCATION IN CONTEXT

LEARNING AT THE WORKPLACE

SOCIAL MEDIA AND ONLINE CO-OPERATION

INNOVATIVE E-LEARNING CONCEPTS

SOCIO-CULTURAL ASPECTS OF E-LEARNING

EMPOWERING THE DIGITAL TEACHER

WHAT'S NEW IN OPEN EDUCATION?

E-LEARNING POLICY AND STRATEGY ISSUES

MOOC PANORAMA

THE DIGITAL LEARNERS' NEEDS AND MOTIVATIONS

ICT ENHANCED LEARNING IN SCHOOLS

INTERNATIONAL E-LEARNING DEVELOPMENT CASES

POSTERS

WORKSHOPS

BOOK OF PROJECTS – COLLECTIONS OF "SYNERGY" SYNOPSES

ICT SUPPORTED COMPETENCE DEVELOPMENT – WHAT DIFFERENCE DOES ICT MAKE?

Cecilia Bjursell, Mohamed Chaib, National Center for Lifelong Learning ENCELL, Jönköping University, Sweden

In the Swedish adult education system, distance education is often presented as a solution for making education flexible and available to all learners. As a supporting device, ICT has been reported to enhance peoples' ability to develop capacity for learning and hence for professional competence development. In this contribution, we intend to scrutinize the veracity behind this assertion. Within the framework of the Swedish National Center for Lifelong Learning (ENCELL) we have been involved in several research and evaluation projects were ICT, in different forms, has been applied. We will take a closer look at two of these projects.

In the first project ITiS (ICT in School) the Swedish Government initiated a huge competence development of about 70 000 teachers in Swedish schools between the years 1999-2003. The main objective of this initiative was to develop new forms of cooperative learning with the support of ICT.

In the second project ECIL (European Certificate in Intergenerational Learning), the five European participating countries developed a distance education program that would be available in their home countries. A special focus on generational issues connected to ICT was addressed.

Out of the empirical evidences observed in these two research and evaluation projects we intend to review:

1. the distinction between the workplace related and the workplace situated competence development when ICT as a learning device is involved, and
2. if and how ICT as a tool for competence development contributed to make any difference for the outcome of learning for the individual learner, the working team and the organization.

INCLUSION AND INTEGRATION IN SWEDEN: USING VIDEO CHAT FOR NEW ARRIVALS IN SWEDEN – HOW TO LEARN SWEDISH LIVE WITH SWEDES ONLINE – EASY, FLEXIBLE, INFORMAL, FAST, FUN

Henrik Hansson, William Boman, Albert Jungselius, Stockholm University, Sweden

In a time when immigration often is described as a burden, this study focuses on how the resources brought by the new arrivals could enrich the Swedish society. The basis is an innovative video chat for new arrivals in Sweden and it is potential for language learning and contact between new arrivals and established Swedes. Focus is on the role of innovative information and communication technology (ICT) services including distance education and informal cross-border communication. Demonstration of the newly developed IT-service will be conducted in relation to the following issues:

- How can the language diversity of the new arrivals be utilized as a resource?
- How can a purpose built video-Internet system facilitate the integration of new arrivals?
- What incentives need to be developed to include the Swedes and the local community?
- What kind of ethical guidelines need to be applied regarding integrity and how open the personal data should be in a specially designed ICT system for new arrivals?
- How can innovative ICT systems shorten the time for new arrivals to get internships and work in Sweden?

The e-service, www.snackasvenska.nu ("chat in Swedish now") are constructed with: (a) safe and secure log in, (b) filter-search mechanisms (such as females can search and be matched only with female speakers, etc.), (c) a lingo point system (more speaking time = more points; new Swedes can show how much time the spoken to Swedes and Swedes can show how much they contributed), (d) a topic box of random speaking themes, (e) a text chat with auto translation from speakers mother tongue to speaking partners mother tongue and more features. The system has been tested with new arrivals/new Swedes – Swedes in Gotland. A demo will be given and results presented at the conference.

SETTING THE TONE: DEVELOPING EFFECTIVE AND CULTURALLY SENSITIVE LEARNING RESOURCES TO IMPROVE THE INTEGRATION PROCESS OF MIGRANTS IN FRANCE

Simon Carolan, Christine Vaufrey, MOOC & Cie, France

Context

Managing mass migration has been subject to great debate in the past few years, notably in light of the recent economic crisis, armed conflicts and changes in the geopolitical sphere. Migration is both a source of richness and a subject of conflict for the countries that welcome migrants.

The cultural and economic benefits of such migration are highly documented. However, due to a lack of understanding of migration on a local, national and international level, overwhelming misconceptions that are overemphasised by social media and the wariness that can exist when the cultural practices of a country's citizens and incoming migrants is diagonally opposed, the integration process of migrants is hindered by tensions.

Providing migrants with tailored educational resources can allow them to better understand the environment within which they find themselves, to recognise the specificities of that environment, comprehend the complexity of the given society and in some cases provide them with arguments in order to anticipate and respond to potential conflictual situations.

Contribution

The MOOC Vivre en France, vivre ensemble (Living in France, living together) addresses the question of smoothening the integration process for migrants in France. We will explore how this MOOC was developed in order to respond to the needs of migrants through a considerable amount of planning in terms of both editorial and production practices.

We will explore the course context and structure in order to demonstrate the importance of finding the right tone, managing the content at learner disposal and handling the distribution process before emitting some recommendations in maintaining an optimal production process faced with the multiple validation processes that such politically sensitive courses with multiple stakeholders are subjected to.

JOIN OUR WORK WITH E-SKILLS, E-WORK AND E-LEARNING!

Torbjörn Skarin, National Organisation for e-competence, Sweden

The National Organization for e-competence (REK) is a Swedish knowledge network that focuses on the development and use of e-skills, e-working, e-learning, e-healthcare and e-government. We are committed to supporting the development of our society, through digitization. REK is a network of Information and Communication (ICT) experts, researchers and investigators, training and education development experts, process and business leaders. REK provides a venue for dialogues, explorative conversations and change. We organize seminars and round table discussions about current and challenging issues, where everyone has a voice. We initiate working groups with the purpose to discuss and analyze the current problems, with a view to find out what needs to be done.

Globalization brings challenges that can best be met with relevant e-skills. Globally there is an increasing need for such skills but the supply does not meet the demand. There is an imbalance between where the supply of e-skilled labour force is geographically located and where it's needed most. The primary and secondary education in many countries have started using digital tools on a limited scale but this needs to reinforced and pedagogical methods developed to meet the needs for e-skills and improve the efficiency of the learning services. There is a need to reinforce the integration of ICT in learning. More individuals need to acquire ICT related competencies and e-skill required by the labour market as well as for people to cope with a rapidly changing world. This could be achieved through improved educational and training methods and by introducing different digitalized learning solutions such as MOOCs, and various forms of online learning.

One advantage of using digital tools in education and training is that they enable cooperation, better communication and ways for teachers and students to track the progress of the learners. Today learners increasingly find it natural to complement and simplify their learning by using more flexible digital tools and venues. New approaches to education and training will also be required to improve the efficiency of learning.

During the past few years REK has made inventories of methods, approaches and tools for provision of ICT related competences and e-skills as well as for language learning. The latter in anticipation of a growing demand for immigrants to learn Swedish.

Given that about 160.000 people applied for asylum in Sweden in 2015, REK realized that this group of new arrivals will need support of flexible learning platforms and digital learning materials that can handle learners with variety of educational and cultural backgrounds. Until recently, only part of those granted asylum have been able to participate in language learning based on the "Swedish for Immigrants"/SFI program. In the latter part of 2015 the Swedish government allocated SEK 133 millions to the project "Swedish from day one". However this does not reach out to all the tens of thousands of asylum seekers living in accommodation arranged by the Swedish Migration Board or municipalities even though it is widely recognized that working skills in Swedish language increases the chances for employment and facilitates inclusion in the society. Skilled employees in many occupational sectors can be found among the newly arrived immigrants, but the use of their skills is prevented by the fact that these individuals do not have sufficient knowledge of Swedish.

In view of the above, REK would like to initiate a collaboration project. This project will study and evaluate flexible approaches to education and training, focusing, initially, on language training. This means that learning will occur both in the classroom, individually or in study groups with using digital tools for language training of newly arrived immigrants and asylum seekers. The project aims to locate good examples of language learning using flexible approaches and digital tools. By presenting and spreading these results to key stakeholders in society, the speed of learning Swedish could be accelerated and the unused skills of foreign-born could come to better use.

CHALLENGE-BASED LEARNING DESIGN IN HIGHER EDUCATION: A NEW CONTEXT FOR LEARNING BEYOND COMPETENCY APPROACH

Loles González, Lluis Pastor, Cristina Girona, Marta Merino, M.B. Palou,
Universitat Oberta de Catalunya, Spain

The Universitat Oberta de Catalunya (Open University of Catalonia, UOC) has launched the PLA-Niu project and it is designed to be a methodological change in the conception of the subjects to be implemented in the entire range of training at the university.

It aims to transform the subjects in the University's programmes into activities designed strictly based on competencies which are aimed at resolving challenges inspired by the professional sphere; to implement a new means of selecting, designing and managing learning resources based on content curation for learning. In the long term, the project affects the entire range of training at the UOC.

A PLA activity is a compact form of training activity, which is defined based on a situation related to a challenge, is competence-based and designed around the activity to be carried out by the student. The acronym PLA stands for "Performance Learning Activity". In addition, Niu contents the training resources and content required to carry out the learning activity successfully organized in a visual aggregator.

The implementation of the PLA-Niu project is based on four guiding elements, which ensure the quality of the process: the project is being driven by the Office of the Vice President for Teaching and Learning, studies of trends in higher education, incremental intervention and personalised and intensive support.

According to the experience of this project, we explain in this paper the conclusions to improve the process in the next phases of work.

LEVEL THE PLAYING FIELD – IMPACT OF ACADEMIC SUCCESS COURSES

Rana Khan, Les Pang, University of Maryland University College, United States of America

The purpose of this research is to evaluate the impact of two "Academic Success Courses", UCSP 635 and UCSP 636, which targets graduate students with little or no programming experience and prepares them for professions that require knowledge and experience in modern computer programming languages. Data representing a total of 14 classes of two preparatory computing courses conducted over three semesters in 2016 were examined. Based on a preliminary analysis of the data, it was discovered that among those who took discipline-specific classes after successfully completing the UCSP courses, about 2/3 of the students received exemplary grades. Those who failed to complete the UCSP courses exhibited a lower level of performance in the program courses. This suggests that the Academic Success Courses has a role in helping students to perform better on the discipline-specific courses. Further research is needed to follow these students through later semesters and to understand the influence of demographics on the course success rate.

ACADEMIC COMMUNICATION VIA TWITTER – THE CASE OF #EDENCHATS

Antonella Poce, Francesco Agrusti, Maria Rosaria Re, Università Roma TRE, Department of Education, Italy

Introduction

The present study tries to offer an overview on the use of Twitter in scholarly communication and will focus on the #EDENchat series, offered on Twitter by EDEN NAP – Network of Academics and Professionals, since 2014.

Individual researchers or Institutions may use twitter for several reasons such as advertising their research, events or publications. The use of correct hashtags increase visibility and may help interaction and exchange of ideas. No fully comprehensive studies exist on how and why scholars use Twitter and some of them highlight how little use of Twitter is made among scholars. The other issue described in the study was related to content. In fact, among those using Twitter, they did not necessarily do so for professional reasons: most of them used it just for personal reasons, in fact. It might be that the above negative attitude is connected to the limitation in characters that Twitter imposes. As we all know, Twitter is a form of free micro-blogging which allows users to send and receive short public messages called tweets. Tweets are limited to no more than 140 characters, and can include links to blogs, web pages, images, videos and all other material online. You can start tweeting anytime, from your computer, smart phone or tablet. By following other people and sources you are able to build up an instant, personalized Twitter feed that meets one's full range of interests, both academic and personal.

The question is: can a just 140 character academic communication has an impact? This paper tries to answer the question, analysing some aspects of #EDENchat series from 2014 up-to-now.

Research Design and Methodology

The #EDENchat discussion series takes place on Twitter periodically, usually in a Wednesday 20:00 (GMT) time slot. #EDENchat is organised and moderated by EDEN NAP steering committee members (Antonella Poce and Steve Wheeler), but increasingly other experts and scholars have been invited to moderate sessions. It regularly attracts participants from across the globe, and discussion is archived via Storify on the EDEN main website. The most recent #EDENchats have featured topics including digital competencies, the future of the university, innovation in teaching, and social media for informal learning.

Mollett, Moran and Dunleavy identify three different tweeting styles: substantive updates, conversational and middle ground. Among the three different tweeting styles identified by the authors #EDENchat series position themselves among the third type, highlighting the more personal and organisational culture into a basically professional approach and most tweets are independently understandable.

Data Analysis

- Statistical analysis: user locations, statistical tweets data, top words in tweets text;
- Sentiment analysis.

Final Remarks

From the analyses carried out, several considerations can be drawn. The first one is related to the impact of the tool, Twitter chat, which helps communication and enhance true interaction among scholars interested in the same subject and located all over the world. On a given appointment they all gather together and discuss about up-to-date topics. Top 100 world cloud highlight that the core issue on which all scholars participating in #edenchats is learning, thinking and students, underlining that there is an objective need to reflect on most effective ways to increase learning for the sake of our students. Sentiment analysis was rather interesting as well and casted light on the positive attitude of field scholars on #edenchats and the subjects discussed.

INVESTIGATING BEHAVIOURS AND ATTITUDES TOWARDS USE OF SOCIAL MEDIA AS A LEARNING TECHNOLOGY AMONG HIGHER EDUCATION STUDENTS IN SAUDI ARABIA

Fatimah Algarni, University of Brighton, United Kingdom

Introduction

Much has been said about the technological, cultural and economic changes brought about by the proliferation of social media into the daily lives of people. Researchers argue that the lives of millennials today are dependent on technology and social media to the extent that their social and cultural practices might be completely different should their digital access be revoked, and that learning today is "an intensely social activity". It is now widely acknowledged that today's students are no longer mere consumers of information but also producers and active participants in the knowledge generation process. All this has led to ample research on the ways in which social media sites and apps have led to a culture of digital connectivity among the neomillenial generation and changed their communication and learning styles. There has also been plenty of research on the ways in which educational institutions can reconsider, reimagine and redesign their pedagogies to encourage more active learning among students by using social media.

Far less has been said however, about the academic impact of social media in conservative societies like Saudi Arabia where the rules of communication and social interactions are completely different from those of Western countries. In such countries where the teacher is viewed as an authority figure who must always be obeyed, and gender segregation is the norm, the extent to which the informal and interactive style of social media sites would work remains to be seen, particularly given that there is very little research that has been conducted on this student segment so far. It is little wonder then that teachers and Universities in Saudi Arabia seem to offer very limited support in terms of social media based learning to students. This research aims to fill some gaps in this area by investigating the current and potential uses, and implications of integrating social media into higher education in Saudi Arabia. The current paper presents the initial results of the work in progress.

Methodology

The main aim of the study is to investigate the current and potential uses, and implications of integrating social media into higher education in Saudi Arabia by exploring the behaviours and attitudes of higher education students in Saudi Arabia towards the use of social media in learning. This requires quantitative and qualitative data. Hence, the research uses a mixed-method research approach following the "Sequential Explanatory Design" to fulfil the research aims. This includes a dominant quantitative strand with surveys as the research instruments, followed by a secondary qualitative strand with interviews as the instruments. Participants are students, teachers and administrators belonging to three Universities in Saudi Arabia: Princess Nourah University, King Saud University and Al-Imam University. A conceptual model has been developed to act as the theoretical guide and provide the context for the study. The model draws references from the theory of Connectivism proposed by Siemens, and is supplemented by the theory of Communities of Practice.

In order to test the validity of the conceptual model, processes and instruments, a pilot survey was conducted with all three groups of participants selected using a convenience sampling technique. Several interesting findings were revealed through the analysis of the pilot survey, indicating that there are considerable gaps between the perceptions of Universities, teachers and students in higher education institutions in Saudi Arabia regarding the use of social media as a learning technology. The findings also revealed certain interesting aspects regarding the usage and attitudes towards academic use of social media that seem unique to students from Saudi Arabia.

Expected Implications

The findings of the study are expected to contribute to the literature in terms of institutional, instructional and student usage of social media as a learning technology in the higher education sector and lay the groundwork for social media policy development among higher educational institutions in Saudi Arabia.

E-VOTING – ENHANCE DIGITAL NATIVE STUDENT INTERACTIONS WITH A NEW VOTING ACTIVITY IN MOODLE

Anne-Dominique Salamin, David Russo, Christophe Hadorn,
University of Applied Sciences Western Switzerland, e-learning Center Cyberlearn, Switzerland

Context

Every year more than 20.000 students enrol in HES-SO different curricula (27% of all Swiss University of Applied Sciences students). The average student age is 25; most students attending a Bachelor curriculum belong to the "digital natives" generation. To behold whether theories dealing with Digital natives can be applied to HES-SO students, the HES-SO e-learning Center Cyberlearn conducted a quantitative study in May 2013, profiling students attending a course at the HES-SO. Survey results indicate that 75% use their smartphones during lectures. Students also express their wish of getting more quizzes, before, during the course. These results give some hints on how much students would like more interactive courses. However, this study shows that only 37% of students would accept to install applications dedicated to learning on their smartphones

E-Voting

Many voting systems help students to more interact during class time (raising hands, clickers, mobile apps). All systems show flaws such as impossibility to use in huge cohorts, unavailability of physical systems, apps installation). As HES-SO offers the LMS Moodle to its professors and students, Cyberlearn decided to embed a new e-voting activity in Moodle, as any other standard Moodle activities. Professors create an e-voting activity in their course space. The activity is used during class time, students can use their computer or their smartphone to read a QR-code, then a web page is displayed on their device. They vote and results appear on a dynamic graph. After the course, professors can access to the previous e-voting activities, sorting it by quiz or by use. The answers remain anonymous. The plug-in has been validated by Moodle community and to date, downloaded more than 800 times. HES-SO professors have created about 540 e-voting activities.

Pedagogical Scenarios of Use

To help professor embed this activity in the teaching process, the full paper proposes three models of application each of them coupled with a pedagogical scenario: the role of initial concepts, the sociological approach: habits linked to social networks and use of the voting activity to sustain the flipped class model.

Conclusion

The voting systems in the classroom or distance learning represent an asset when animating large classes, increasing interactivity, decreasing the participants' disengagement or help the professor to transform the students' initial concepts on the course content. The e-voting activity in Moodle is open source and free, enables a non-intrusive, simple and pleasant way to insert this type of activity in the learning process. The technical evolution used to collect the answers to the questions in the classroom, serves a fundamental pedagogic aim: engaging students to become actors of their own learning transformation. Xenophon, a Greek author born in 430 BC, already claimed at the time: "Asking a question is teaching". An activity such as e-voting for Moodle modernises the process while maintaining its usefulness and its educational wealth.

Contacts

To find out more about e-voting on Moodle, please contact the author (adominique.salamin@hes-so.ch) or Cyberlearn@hes-so.ch.

To download the plug-in (for local platform administrator): https://moodle.org/plugins/mod_evoting

PRE-TERTIARY LEARNING ANALYTICS SYSTEM WHICH SUPPORTS EQUAL OPPORTUNITIES

Blaženka Divjak, Petra Vondra, University of Zagreb, Croatia

In this paper we elaborate the design of pre-production National Learning Analytics (LA) and Data Mining System. Research and reports about LA System (LAS) development lag on both the national (regional) and individual (school) level. The methodology and the approach presented in this paper is developed in the scope of the project "E-schools: Establishing a System for Developing Digitally Mature Schools (pilot project)".

Our approach to the design consists of the following five phases: objectives setting, user needs analysis, data availability analysis, dashboards development (goals settings and defining dashboard functionalities) and specification of the tender.

Identified target groups are: (a) Students/pupils and their parents, (b) Teachers, (c) School management and support (principal/pedagogue/psychologist), (d) Local and national education authority (School founders/ Ministry/Agencies for Quality Assurance), (e) Policy making bodies and researchers and (f) Project partners on "E-schools" project. To increase the usability of LAS the involvement of users is essential and for the student's dashboard it is important to reflect diversity of student body and to support equal opportunity concept. LAS is developed with the bottom-up approach.

The most relevant questions which present students' interest and were gathered during the needs analysis phase are related to comparison of the student's achieved competencies and competencies required in the labour market; comparison of student's achievement and the preconditions for enrolment into secondary school/higher education; teachers' performance; risks students have in achieving their goals; how students can improve their performance; impact of various factors on student's achievement (such as social status of a family, school equipment and design, working atmosphere, school practice, team work, absences from school, time spent on independent work) and the impact of various factors on the achievement of competencies.

Today, teachers face different challenges in classroom and should balance between different requirements from students who are culturally and linguistically diverse, who have different educational background or socio-economic status and students with other disabilities in learning. Concerning learning analytics as a promising tool that can help in assessing and handling diversity in learners' background and performance, we will present in this paper the dashboard for students, developed according to the results of performed needs analysis.

The design process consists of several rounds of user consultations with a special focus on the interests of learners. Consultations start with focus groups and panels followed by the relevance evaluations. Finally, targeted users give feedback on the pre-production functionalities of each dashboard. Altogether 628 representatives of users participated in relevance and assessment phases, of which 164 were primary and secondary schools' students. Further development needs to acknowledge the challenges of collection and protection of data, interpretation of results and continuous adjustment to meet the users' needs. Additionally, LA interventions, by design, must account for the diversity of the student body.

The central part of Learning Analytics System is Data Analysis System. Very important part of the LAS is the Consent System that allows students and teachers finer control of how their personal data is used. The System for Warning and Intervention helps students and teachers to deal with risks, and finally Success Planner enables the development of students' planning competencies and other metacognitive skills. Special consideration is given to supporting diverse student body and providing equal education opportunities for all to ensure effective teaching and learning strategies and access to students' support. Ethical decision making about the design of LAS, as well as the ethical conduct of use of LA are key to this project but also to every LA project that involves children, adolescents, and young adults (presumably unable to give their own informed consent formally at some age) of different socio-economic, ethnic, cultural and religious backgrounds, and from different geographical regions/countries.

ADAPTIVE LEARNING AS A TOOL FOR SUPPORTING DIVERSE STUDENTS WITH THRESHOLD CONCEPTS AT A DISTANCE

Anne-Marie Gallen, Gerald Evans, The Open University, United Kingdom

A key aspect of the learning experience for students is the need to consolidate and absorb what they are learning. To do so, they need space and time, as well as additional support to overcome any aspects of their learning that they find particularly challenging. A number of researchers have identified the idea that *threshold concepts* exist across many subject areas which require students to make a transformative, irreversible and integrative step in their learning.

This paper concentrates on an example of a first level undergraduate engineering module and the challenges of teaching the key mathematical concepts needed to a diverse audience of engineering students with varying levels of mathematical ability.

Evidenced by poor understanding and performance during their second level study, as well as perceptions held by tutors teaching at higher levels, it is clear that *rearranging equations* is a key threshold concept that some students never surmount. In reviewing their findings, the production team settled on the concept of rearranging equations as being the key barrier for many level 1 engineering students.

Having identified the threshold concept, the team worked with the Technology Enhanced Learning department in the university to design prototype solutions that could support students with getting through this threshold.

The paper outlines how the resulting project team went about identifying the threshold concept, planned an adaptive learning approach to supporting students and then discusses the findings from this initial work. We then go on to consider developing the approach for future cohorts of students.

TOWARD A MOBILE OPEN AND SOCIAL LANGUAGE LEARNING PARADIGM

Timothy Read, Elena Barcena, UNED, Spain, John Traxler, University of Wolverhampton, Agnes Kukulska-Hulme, The Open University, United Kingdom

In the SWITCHED-ON project (The empoWerment of maSsive open social language learning through mobile TeCHnology: harnEssing interactions, transcenDing bOuNdaries – this ongoing project is funded by the Spanish Ministry of Economy and Competitiveness (Programa Estatal de Fomento de la Investigación Científica y Técnica de Excelencia, Subprograma Estatal de Generación del Conocimiento; ref. no. FFI2016-80613-P)) the authors are analysing the affordances of open social learning, in the widest sense, for second languages. In this work, mobile technology (including MALL) is conceived to be not just a tool that can be used for undertaking certain tasks (in an unstructured and loosely controlled manner), but as the main way in which second language learners can interact and carry out their learning effectively. The hypothesis underlying the work in this project is that given the complex, hectic and mobile nature of 21st century societies, open social language learning can take place with a backbone defined by mobile technology. This will represent a new paradigm that is both inclusive for a wider range of language learners than is the case with current open online courses, and is more effective, since it blurs the boundaries of everyday life with learning. It is envisaged that this will happen through the combination of mobile online interaction with integrated supportive MALL practices. The emergence of MOOCs was as an important step forward in providing open education, including foreign languages, to the large number of people who, for diverse reasons, are not able to attend conventional taught classes or participate in closed online courses. However, given the current diversity of LMOOCs, the authors argue that it is more appropriate to be thinking in terms of open social language learning in general, since there are many different ways to harness existing technology to facilitate second language learning (2LL) which includes but goes beyond the standard MOOC formats, and that the boundaries between what is a course and what is not, are not always so clear or relevant. Previous experiences of the authors with different types of LMOOCs have let us identify their potential problems. However, 2LL can be seen to be eminently practical and dynamic, and as such, falls in the middle of the scale of 'intrinsic MOOC suitability', since it is both skill-based and knowledge-based. This requires a network of capabilities (competences, skills and data) to be finely intertwined as learning progresses. Such learning requires both cognitive involvement (using high-order mental skills) and social interaction (with more or less competent speakers of the target language). Experience gained so far is enabling the concept to be refined empirically, by focusing on what works best, in terms of factors like the average number of hours a course requires, the prototypical profile of the students, etc., as well as basic instructional design issues such as selecting suitable methodology and supporting technology (where options are available). However, regardless of the conceptual and terminological confusion related to these courses, experience shows that they are popular with students, in terms of their numbers, course statistics and student/teacher satisfaction. Arguably, the popularity comes in part from the lack of associated cost and the flexibility of access and commitment that MOOCs offer. Unlike other initiatives related to OERs (Open Educational Resources), the essential learner-centeredness and social orientation of these courses are also generally found to be both stimulating and rewarding by the students. Formats are still being explored, intense CPD (Continuing Professional Development) being seen as optimal. The authors' work in SWITCHED-ON aims at exploring the conceptual space of MALL and open social 2LL and how the affordances of mobile technology can empower their combination for large student numbers. However, regardless of the benefits of using mobile devices with such courses, to enrich the learning process and extend it into peoples' everyday lives away from the limited time they have access to desktop computers, it is still the case that mobile access is desired first and foremost because it reflects the way people live today, and will arguably facilitate the use of such courses for people who do not have access to other means. In the authors' experience, 2LL is most effective when a scaffolded spiral approach is used, moving people from teacher-led to self-directed learning, and back again; combining an individual learning stage with subsequent social-constructivist ones. In the case of LMOOCs, teachers are not typically present once the course starts to adapt the activities to the progress of the learner. Therefore, the paradigm developed in this project is intended to be applied to plot the possible learning paths of individual open social language learning courses and provide adequate and relevant scaffolding. Indeed, there are many ways in which learning scenarios can be structured to move people through the LMOOC, back and forth to and from the real world, using mobile technology, so further research is needed to explore and theorise about the space of possible conceptual designs.

COLLABORATIVE ONLINE LEARNING AT A DISTANCE – A CASE STUDY AND DEVELOPING THE KNOWLEDGE BASE

Gerald Evans, Daphne Chang, The Open University, United Kingdom

The pedagogical benefits of collaborative activity have been well recognised. It helps students to develop critical thinking skills, reflective abilities, team working skills and enable transformative learning by co-creation of knowledge. For subjects that require students to "... examine, assess and synthesise multiple perspective to resolve ill-structure problem", collaborative activity is seen as an integral part of teaching. Over the years, educators at The Open University (OU) have developed sophisticated online virtual laboratories, gamification and animation opportunities and a suite of tools to choose from to deliver and support collaborative online activities. However, academic teams at the OU continue to face many challenges in designing, delivering and supporting successful online collaborative activities.

In seeking to better support academic teams with delivery and support for online collaborative activities, the TEL Design team at The Open University produced a guide to good practice on collaborative online activities last year. This guide explains the purposes of online collaborative activities and makes explicit why they are beneficial. It outlines that we can deliver effective collaborative online activities by understanding the impact of online collaboration, making activities meaningful, paying attention to/catering for diversity and careful design and using appropriate tools for collaboration. It also provides exemplars on guidance for students, tutor support and assessing students' online collaboration.

This paper looks at a specific case study of how the good practices outlined in this guide can be used to achieve enhanced collaborative experience for learners with different social-cultural backgrounds and personal circumstances. We will also examine how some of the findings can be aligned with key studies in the field. Lastly, we will conclude by talking about the future of collaborative online learning at our institution and how we feel we can evolve our approaches based on the improved understanding we have developed through our work.

A MATTER OF DISTANCE – STEPPING INTO THE "DANCE" OF PRACTICE THROUGH EPORTFOLIOS

Susan Sherringham, UTS:Insearch, Australia

The overarching project under consideration in this paper is that of supporting international students to transition into university culture in Australia through the development of knowledge, skills and dispositions. In this context the concept of distance shifts from distance learning to *distance load* where students face many levels of distance in their transition to university. This paper suggests that a reconceptualization of ePortfolios through practice theory may prove useful in addressing distance load. An ePortfolio reconceptualised as rehearsal and performance space, a supportive environment where students can metaphorically step in and out of the "dance" of learning, offers a conceptual frame for a personal journey, an apprenticeship into new ways of knowing, doing, and being, and an acculturation into practices and learning communities. It is proposed that by engaging with curriculum through an ePortfolio, informed by social practice theory, students not only develop skills and knowledge, but also more evolved dispositions that begin to embody technology as a valued and integral part of learning in a way that can be carried forward into their social and civic life. In conceiving of educational practice, through the lens of practice theory, it is posited that the skills and knowledge (required) to actively engage in a society (characterized by digital technology) are learned and embodied through practices

DECOLONISATION OF THE CURRICULUM AS A PLEA FOR MEANINGFUL LEARNING: STRATEGIES FOR DISTANCE EDUCATION TEACHING AND LEARNING BASED ON MIND, BRAIN, AND EDUCATION SCIENCE

Ignatius G.P. Gous, University of South Africa, South Africa

The call for the decolonization of the curriculum has grown into a world-wide movement and phenomenon. It speaks to the heart of education, calling into question the character and essence of what universities and other institutions of education and learning are, present and do. In this position paper, definitions of the concept of decolonization are explored based on a literature review. On the basis of an understanding, the core concept is seen not so much as a political issue, but a plea for meaningful learning. Meaningful learning is an important aspect of Mind Brain and Education Science, which is being explored and explained. Following from this, a program is suggested on how this aspect of learning could be incorporated in the curriculum, making it part and parcel of teaching and learning in 21st century institutions of teaching and learning

The Concept of Decolonization

Decolonisation is a very nebulous concept being used to refer to anything from indigenisation to political activism, with many shades of meanings in between. This very cursory overview uses the text mining tool Leximancer © to identify themes in the literature. It is not intended to be an exhaustive description, but aims at identifying some common basis underlying the quests the term is made part of. To my mind, it is al addressing experiences of alienation, therefore being pleas for meaningful learning which could help learners to address issues pertinent and important to them and their contexts.

Meaningful Learning as defined by Mind, Brain, and Education Science

The quest for meaningful learning has a long history in teaching and learning. This paper, however, approaches it from the vantage point of the Mind. Brain, and Education Sciences, which is an interdisciplinary science combining insights from Neurology, Cognitive Science and Pedagogy. One goal of these sciences is to identify effective learning strategies, and some of these strategies focus on application to real life contexts. Understanding the theories undergirding this, it forms the basis of practical teaching and learning strategies, which is ultimately useable. The theory underlying this section are mainly that of neuroconstructivism as formulated by Annette Karmiloff-Smith, but reference is also made to the theory of Bronfenbrenner's ecological theory.

Meaningful Learning in Action: A Program and an Agenda

Academic theories are intended to address real life situations, but sometimes they are not carried over into practice, or they are not heard by practitioners. This article refers to a program based on MBE Science, but which is used in practice especially by distance education students and lecturers.

The 2030 Development Goals underscore the importance of self-directed, life-long learners. This is seen as of particular interest to students at Distance Education institutions, and especially to people in the workplace after completion of their formal studies which continues to the end of their careers and even thereafter. Recent developments at universities worldwide, but especially in South Africa under the current #fallist movements, pushed the importance of this to the fore particularly to students at traditional contact universities who were unpreparedly forced to cope without being guided during classes and having to study online at a distance. Many students reporting that they find this difficult.

The question is therefore how people can be prepared to become self-directed life-long learners, prepared for learning under all circumstances. This article provides an overview of what effective learning entails, seen from the perspective of the Mind, Brain, and Education Sciences. The implications of these findings are then translated into an agenda for teaching and learning by educators of all institutions, and a practical program for students, all of whom are unexpectedly being pushed into the role of Distance Educators and Distance Education students as the result of campus unrest.

THE IMPORTANCE OF OPENNESS WITHIN DIGITAL LITERACY

Fabio Nascimbeni, Universidad Internacional de la Rioja (UNIR), Brazil

The paper argues that in order to support the necessary holistic understanding of Digital Literacy, one needs to take into account the change in knowledge production, management and consumptions that we have been witnessing in the last couple of decades, mainly connected with the pervasiveness of ICT and with the raise of social online practices. In an increasingly connected society where sharing is becoming in many cases the norm, we consider that a fundamental component of Digital Literacy should be *the capacity to work in the open*, sharing beyond our circles the knowledge we produce and making use of knowledge produced by others, in a transparent and traceable way. We cannot dream of open societies, open innovation and open education if we do not acquire the basic capacity to adopt open approaches in our daily activities: acquiring these basic capacities means becoming openness literate.

In order to understand whether (and to which extent) *openness-related competences* are included in existing Digital Literacy approaches, the paper briefly analyses two well-known Digital Literacy frameworks: the one by JISC, the UK national agency in charge of ICT in education, and the one from the Mozilla Foundation – a pioneering institution working on the relation between internet and society. We have been looking for the potential impact of these frameworks in developing the capacity to work in the open, by searching for the way each component of the frameworks (being a skill, an area of activity, or something else) is thereby declined in terms of sharing, open licensing etc. The first conclusion is that the two frameworks are fully in line with the holistic understanding of Digital Literacy that is required to build active and participative citizens.

Such a holistic view of Digital Literacy is particularly important in the education field, where using ICT can be understood as both instrumental to general learning purposes and as an area of reflection per-se. Along these lines, we argue that being able to *work in the open* should not only be a fundamental literacy requirement for citizens, but also a prerequisite for teachers at all educational levels, especially if we want our schools to work in a connected way, learning across cultures and through collaboration.

An important recent development in this domain is the DigCompEdu project by the Joint Research Centre of the European Commission in Seville, which aims to develop a digital competence framework for educators at European level, with the aim to inform and reinforce national initiatives in the field under a common umbrella. The DigCompEdu is an important step in the right direction for stakeholders to understand the importance of embedding openness as a key feature of collaboration within Digital Literacy practices. Still, research need to further inform present and future policies in this evolving field, along three interrelated dimensions of literacy practice: an *operational dimension* that includes the skills and competences that enable individuals to read, write and interact across a range of platforms, tools and media, a *sociocultural dimension* that refers to developing a repertoire of digital literacy practices in specific social and cultural contexts, and a *critical dimension* that recognises that meaning-making resources are selective and often operate as a means of social control and social exclusion.

In conclusion, we argue that contemporary Digital Literacy initiatives, building on efforts such as the ones by JISC, Mozilla or the European Commission, should aim at transforming citizens – and educators – into critically literate actors able not simply to participate competently in digital practices but also to transform these practices actively and creatively, in a collaborative and open way.

THE POWER OF FEEDBACK IN ONLINE LEARNING: HOW TO INCORPORATE INTERCULTURAL INTELLIGENCE WHEN COMMUNICATING EVALUATIVE COMMENTS

Hyoshin Kim, University of British Columbia, Canada

How do cultural differences impact the way we give and receive feedback in online learning environments? The goal of this paper is to explore: (a) the notion of intercultural intelligence; and (b) culturally appropriate and effective ways of using feedback. Cultural norms and expectations vary widely in communicating evaluative messages. This paper focuses on recent literature on theories and practice that address relevant skills and understanding required for enhancing informal and formal feedback in online learning environments. The main focus of the paper is to examine how cultural and contextual factors influence communicating feedback. A key objective of this exploration is to understand different norms around power relations, face giving and saving, communication styles such as high and low context, and identities. In addition, the literature review portion will include some of the latest research on feedback, communication and sociolinguistic ideologies. The main purpose of the paper is not prescriptive, but collaborative and exploratory.

Whether we are aware of it or not, we are constantly involved in exchanging and responding to feedback in personal and professional settings. Our social life is filled with feedback: performance reviews, program evaluations, proposal comments, nonverbal communication, online and offline meetings, etc. Feedback plays a significant role in our everyday life as it affects our behaviour, decision making, and relations. The results of feedback are essential for learning and can have lasting impacts on identities, relations and attitudes. Current literature provides useful insights into the importance of feedback.

However it fails to recognize its complexity as a unique form of communication and often ignores key cultural differences around managing feedback. The biggest mistake in handling feedback stems from the assumption of similarities. For example, clear and explicit delineation of what is wrong with someone's work can be regarded as a true sign of deep respect in certain contexts. However, the same can be interpreted as rude, offensive, demotivating and humiliating in others. This is because people do not hold exactly the same beliefs, customs and expectations. In technology-mediated learning environments, non-verbal cues and other contextual factors add another level of complexity in communicating feedback

As our workplace becomes increasingly globalized, we need to understand and develop culturally appropriate and effective feedback skills that empower others and achieve results. In online learning environments, collaborative learning and effective feedback communication play a crucial role in affecting student participation, engagement and learning outcomes. By drawing on recent research on the notion of growth mindset and intercultural competence, we will be able to consider innovative ways to create more inclusive online learning. This paper examines Eurocentric tendencies reflected in research and incorporates studies that involve non-Western value systems. The paper includes suggestions on how to:

- identify different theoretical models and research on feedback;
- apply cultural and contextual approaches to giving and receiving feedback;
- build trust and credibility across cultures; and
- harness technology to achieve culturally appropriate and effective communication

The literature review offers perspectives from a variety of disciplines, such as psychology, anthropology, and intercultural communication, and insights into the role of culture in technology-mediated communication with respect to feedback.

FROM FRONTIER LEARNING TO BLENDED COMMUNITY LEARNING: A PHENOMENOGRAPHY OF INFORMAL LEARNING IN RURAL COMMUNITY INFORMATICS

Catherine Helen Arden, University of Southern Queensland, Australia

In Australia, in spite of a policy commitment at the national level to an investment in national broadband internet infrastructure across the country, the problem of an enduring digital divide – along with the probability of an associated learning divide – persists, particularly for so-called disadvantaged groups in rural and regional communities. Therefore, like their counterparts in many countries around the world, Australian rural communities are working on strategies to build the capacity of their citizens for active participation "in an information society that includes a concept of civil society as a target for skills development, engagement, decision-making, and societal cohesion". Such strategies include the Learning Communities movement, in which towns, cities, and communities adopt a "learning-based approach to community development with a framework in which lifelong learning is the organising principle and social goal" and grass-roots community technology (Community Informatics) initiatives that seek to leverage digital Information Communications Technologies (ICTs) and the Internet in the interests of supporting the achievement of community development and digital inclusion goals. One such initiative is GraniteNet, established in 2006 in the town of Stanthorpe in South-East Queensland with the aim of harnessing the possibilities presented by digital technologies and the Internet for enhanced social connectivity, community networking, and citizen engagement in lifelong and life-wide learning.

The author concurs with Merriam et al. that "informal learning contexts, including social action and community-based learning, are where much of adult learning takes place (and that as adult educators and researchers) we need only see them as sites for learning" to be able to explore and better understand, and make visible, the dynamics and complexity of this learning. Using phenomenography as the primary research approach, the author explored the experience of learning with a purposive sample of 20 community volunteers drawn from among GraniteNet's diverse communities and networks of interest and practice at a high point in the organisation's development in 2012. Although learning across various content domains was explored, particular emphasis is given to the interrogation of conceptions and experiences of learning about and learning to use digital technologies in GraniteNet's face-to-face, virtual and hybrid community learning and working environments. Phenomenographic analysis of interview transcripts and respondent-generated mind maps identified seven qualitatively distinct, yet logically related ways of experiencing learning in GraniteNet, representing the collective learning consciousness of GraniteNet at the time of the study. This constituted the study's outcome space, which is interpreted in the context of the case study description to illuminate the experience of learning in GraniteNet and to theorise about the nature and dynamics of this learning.

The study's findings confirm those reported in the literature on learning in associational life and volunteer work that emphasise the variety of learning opportunities afforded by small-scale voluntary and community-based organisations "across the spectrum of adult learning" along with the breadth, depth and significance of this learning for participants. They also demonstrate how individual and collective learning is further expanded through the "combination of digital interactions with offline encounters" afforded by GraniteNet's hybrid socio-technical working and learning environments. Related to this are new understandings and insights generated about informal learning as a phenomenon linked to younger and older adults' growing capacity for metacognition and reflexivity in the interests of understanding and furthering their own learning, providing evidence to support the assertion that, under the right conditions, digital technology can be used to "support sustainable environments where learners gain new perspectives on their learning, share and learn collectively, and master their own drive for learning".

DIVERSITY: A BLESSING OR A CURSE FOR ONLINE COLLABORATION?

Francisca Frenks, XWebinar.nl and www.dyhme.com, the Netherlands, Gizeh Perez-Tenorio, Linköping University, Miriam Mosing, Mohammed Seed Ahmed, Karolinska Institute, Natalia Rivera Sifaki, Karolinska Institute and Karolinska University Hospital, Sweden, Sonja Sharp, Varsity College Cape Town, South Africa, Åsa Kneck, Ersta Sköndal University, Sweden

The authors, independently and without any prior knowledge of each other, joined a learning experiment: the Open Networked Learning (ONL162) course for several months in the autumn of 2016. We were randomly assigned to the same Problem Based Learning (PBL) group and collaborated 100% online. Our group, PBL9, was part of a Community of Inquiry, (COI) consisting of more than 100 students and 25 facilitators. We worked synchronously and asynchronously.

Learn to collaborate online in diverse groups matters because complex challenges in today's society ask for smart solutions. Smart solutions can only be achieved when 1 + 1 = 3, when people, with diverse knowledge, experience and perspectives collaborate. When synergy is created out of diversity, when people learn to collaborate effectively and happy.

Was diversity a curse or a blessing for PBL9, our group? We were diverse, yet there was commonality as well. How did we balance between togetherness and diversity? We want to share our experience and the knowledge we gained with the participants of #EDEN17.

We will answer these questions in our paper:

1. Why does collaboration and diversity matter?
2. What do we mean by diversity?
3. When was diversity a curse? When was it a blessing?
4. What is the role of the individual group members for happy online and collaborative learning?
5. What is the role of the facilitator and co-facilitator?
6. What kind of diversity matters the most in our educational context?

We believe diversity matters when collaborating in an educational context, as it brings to the group the "multi-perspectiveness" that is needed when looking at complex problems. Further we will provide tips to make online collaboration with a diverse group a blessing.

Contact

e-mail: francisca@xwebinar.nl or gizeh.perez-tenorio@liu.se

THE VIRTUAL CLASSROOM FOR EDUCATIONAL ACTIVITIES: UNDERSTANDING INFRASTRUCTURES FOR LEARNING

Giulia Messina Dahlberg, Anita Kjellström, University of Skövde, Sweden

Online learning is a reality for higher educational institutions around the globe. Since the beginning of the 21st century, many universities in Sweden have begun to offer online courses at a variety of levels completely online, including synchronous meetings. This study aims to contribute by investigating (a) how space, in terms of educational infrastructure with a range of affordance for learning, is co-created by the participants in a open online course and (b) how a range of activities are mutually shaped by the course design and by the learning space(s) where the course is offered. The data we focus upon come from project KSLL (combination course for students and lifelong learning) and consist of recordings of online seminars from a course in Pedagogy in higher education. The seminars were conducted through Adobe Connect, a multimodal environment which offers synchronous oral communication, with cameras for (limited) access to paralinguistic cues, and textchat. Students' texts and the transcriptions of the asynchronous discussions in the course homepage are part of the data along with the course homepage, as well as tracking of the social media presence of the course in Facebook and Twitter. By using an (n)ethnographic approach, the analysis highlights the ways in which learning spaces as infrastructure shape and are shaped by the range of activities that are part of the course, but also by the openness of the space itself, which affords the emergence of alternative pathways for participation and thus, we argue, for learning.

DROPOUT IN AN ONLINE TRAINING FOR IN-SERVICE TEACHERS

Klaus D. Stiller, Regine Bachmaier, University of Regensburg, Germany

High dropout rates are still a problem with online training. The phenomenon appears to be complex, depending on numerous factors. The literature suggests that learner characteristics influence the decision to persist in an online course or to drop out. Domain-specific prior knowledge is known to influence program usage, information processing and performance. Students having higher prior knowledge can more easily study because of having less new information connected to prior knowledge. Consequently, learners might experience a lower level of workload and be less threatened by learning difficulties. Thus, the level of prior knowledge might influence a learner's decision to drop out. Motivation is one of the most frequently studied variables in relation to dropout, and it has been shown to be correlated to course persistence and dropout. A student's greater involvement in deeper learning might contribute to reduced dropout rates. Metacognitive strategies, time management and creating a supporting learning environment are considered to be particularly relevant for online learning. Higher levels of these learning skills might contribute to reducing dropout. Studies have shown that management skills are significant predictors of dropout, especially managing time effectively and having comfortable conditions for studying. Computer attitude and anxiety might also influence a learner's decision to drop out by affecting learning. Negative computer attitudes and computer anxiety might disturb learning because of negative emotions and thoughts associated with the computer. The limited studies investigating the effects of computer attitudes on course dropout have found a significant relation between positive attitudes on course usage and persistence. Studies about computer anxiety showed mixed results.

An online training in media pedagogy for in-service teachers was used to explore course dropout. We examined whether student dropout is influenced by prior knowledge, intrinsic motivation, learning strategies, computer attitude, and computer anxiety by simply comparing the learner characteristics in the identified groups of dropout learners and persistent learners. We assumed that dropout is more likely when a learner has a lower level of prior knowledge, intrinsic motivation as well as learning skills, more negative attitudes towards computers, and a higher level of computer anxiety.

The data was collected from 318 in-service teachers who enrolled in a vocational online training about media education. The training addressed teachers of primary schools, secondary general schools, intermediate schools and grammar schools in the German Federal State of Bavaria. The online modular training was based on instructional texts without a fixed schedule. Before starting the training, the participants were asked to provide demographic information and to respond to various items that assessed learner characteristics. A prior-knowledge test was presented before each module, and after completing the module, participants completed a final module test.

More female than male teachers enrolled in the training. The mean age of teachers was about 40 years. Most teachers worked in an intermediate school. A dropout rate of 50.0% was observed. Two groups were formed: (a) dropout students who only registered (n = 63) and students who started learning but failed to complete any of the course modules (n = 96) and (b) studying students who completed at least one module (n = 159). The dropout group appeared to be older and more male than female. They also possessed less prior knowledge, metacognitive skills and skills to arrange an adequate learning environment. No differences were found in type of school, intrinsic motivation, computer attitude, and computer anxiety between dropouts and studying students. Generally, only small effects were found.

No explanation for the age and sex differences emerged in this study. In contrast to the literature, successful learners in this study appear to be younger than dropout students. Our results pertaining to learning skills, however, are in line with former research on learning performance and learning management skills, but we did not find that time management was essential in contradiction to other studies. Overall, computer attitude and computer anxiety were not indicative of dropping out. This result is not consistent with evidence from other studies. In general, the act of dropping out remains a complex phenomenon. Our results suggest that various learner characteristics are connected to dropping out. Although readers should be careful in generalizing the results, learning management skills seem to be a good starting point to set up interventions against dropping out. Other features, such as age and sex, could inform educators as to whom an effective intervention should be offered when a threat of dropping out is detected.

SECONDARY TEACHING AT A DISTANCE: A NEW ZEALAND CASE STUDY

Kwok-Wing Lai, University of Otago, New Zealand

This paper reports findings of a case study investigating how distance online teaching was supported in New Zealand at the secondary level. 48 teachers from NetNZ, a cluster of schools offering online courses to distance students, participated in this study in 2016. As part of a larger project investigating the pedagogical and cultural practices of New Zealand online teachers, this study investigated specifically (a) why New Zealand teachers engaged in distance teaching and how they felt about teaching online; and (b) what professional development and learning was needed to support and sustain online teaching. The respondents completed an online questionnaire containing 44 closed and open-ended questions. Both quantitative and qualitative analyses were conducted. The quantitative analyses were primarily descriptive, although analyses on group differences based on gender and teaching experience were also conducted. Thematic analyses were conducted on the qualitative data.

Findings of this exploratory study showed that while almost all the NetNZ teachers enjoyed online teaching, only a small proportion of them indicating a strong preference for online teaching, and a few of them felt that they were particularly successful in online teaching as compared to on-site classroom teaching. There was a clear gender difference in online and technology using experience, with female teachers being less experienced than male teachers. However, the lack of technology using experience did not seem to be a barrier for the female teachers to teach online. In terms of why teachers engaged in online teaching, while institutional pressure in terms of the need to provide students with more course options and increasing class sizes were important factors, proportionally more teachers in this study provided personal reasons such as the willingness of stepping out from one's comfort zone to develop different teaching skills as a major reason for engaging in online teaching. These reasons may have implications for future recruitment of online teachers. For the NetNZ teachers, they were keen to learn how to develop their classes as a learning community, develop learning materials, and how to develop their students as self-regulated and independent learners. Support on how to assess online students should be provided for beginning online teachers. For future professional development, most NetNZ teachers preferred to attend workshops run by experts, although they were also keen to participate in an ongoing community of practice. While less experienced teachers would like to work with an expert teacher on a one-to-one basis, more experienced teacher would like to take part in regular face-to-face peer-supported group discussions as a form of professional development.

ROADMAP FOR THE FUTURE OF OPEN EDUCATION IN AUSTRALIA

Sandra Wills, Charles Sturt University, Shirley Alexander, University of Technology Sydney, David Sadler, University of Tasmania, Australia

Australia has a long history in open education both as an early pioneer and in delivery at scale. Looking back over the changing definitions, changing channels and changing purposes provides a landscape for consideration of new directions in Australian open education. Open has morphed through three phases: free of location or time constraints; free of pre-requisites; free of cost.

The first two phases were supported and facilitated by Australian government strategy and substantial funding for Australian universities. So far, the third phase has no vision or backing at the national level. Whilst the Australian government has put resources and support behind its aspiration to facilitate open access and reuse of Australia's publicly funded *research* resources via the Australian Government's Open Access and Licensing Framework, the reform process has not significantly moved to embrace *educational* resources.

In 2014, the Australian Government Office for Learning and Teaching funded a national project called OpenEdOz [see website openedoz.org] which produced a roadmap for national policy in open education for Australian universities. The project involved the three partner institutions above, plus a reference group and an evaluator, who were OEP experts recognised nationally and internationally.

The project conducted think tanks and sourced case studies which provided signposts for national action. A Theme Matrix was developed with initial themes derived from international literature and projects on OER policy including 2012 Paris OER Declaration (2012), Commonwealth of Learning (2015), Policies for OER Uptake project (POERUP, 2014), and Open Education Quality Initiative (2011). The top 11 OEP themes that emerged from this analysis were: Student Voice, Institutional Strategy, National Policy, Student Co-creation, Course offered as OER, Degree design based on OER, Modules based on OER, Credit Transfer, Accreditation of informal & non-formal learning, Open Licensing and Open Textbooks.

From the case studies, twenty-five individual strategies that could contribute to national action were provided in the final OpenEdOz National Roadmap which has ten signposts: Awareness, Students, Teachers, Standards, IP & Copyright, ICT Infrastructure, Research, Discoverability, Collaboration and Sustainability.

The National Roadmap is intended to directly support the Australia federal government to take advantage of the full potential of Open Education for the Australian higher education sector. The project team hopes that this Roadmap will further inform national level decision makers of the issues to consider while engaging with Open Educational Practices. We also hope this roadmap will encourage the development of OEP focused policies and regulations at national levels, so that the Australian higher education will be able to fully take advantage of the already globally recognised opportunities of OEP. In the meantime, a number of national education bodies have been invited to become fully engaged as drivers of Australia's Open Education Strategy for universities.

Acknowledgement

In addition to the co-authors who as university senior executives lead the project, the OpenEdOz team comprised Dr. Carina Bossu, Associate Professor Natalie Brown, Janet Chelliah, Dr. Peter Kandlbinder, Associate Professor Philip Uys; Katherine Klapdor, Linda Ward. Reference Group comprised Dr. Irwin Devries, Canada; Sarah Lambert, Australia; Professor Megan Quentin-Baxter, United Kingdom/Australia; Dr. Sarah Porter, United Kingdom; Professor Wayne Mackintosh, New-Zealand. External evaluator: Grainne Conole, United Kingdom.

TOWARDS PRIVACY ISSUES IN PERSONAL LEARNING ENVIRONMENTS – A CONCEPTUAL MODEL OF PLE PRIVACY

Malinka Ivanova, TU Sofia, Bulgaria, Victoria Marín, Universität Oldenburg, Germany, Institut de Recerca e Innovació Educativa (IRIE), Universitat de les Illes Balears, Spain, Gemma Tur, Universitat de les Illes Balears, Spain, Ilona Buchem, Beuth Hochschule für Technik Berlin, Germany

Introduction and Research Questions

Personal Learning Environments (PLE) as an approach to technology enhanced learning emphasizes the shift of control and ownership from the educator or the designer of a learning environment to the user or the learner, bestowing decision making and choice upon the learner, especially the choice of the learning tools and the use of these tools for learning. According to this approach each learner designs a unique learning environment to support and enhance individual learning, collecting a wide variety of personal data related not only to the private life, but also to the student learning profile. While more and more private data is created and shared on the Internet, more and more enterprises, government agencies and marketers are collecting personal data. Many users and learners are not aware of how their private data is used or misused and they are not taking steps to protect their personal data from being used by others. At the same time, it is possible to use the data created and shared on the Internet for educational purposes, for example by means of learning analytics and recommender systems to support individual learning processes. By addressing the problem of privacy in Personal Learning-Environments in this paper, we are focusing on privacy of ordinary and sensitive data in context of digital, social learning. The emerging research questions are:

- What kind of personal data is required to support organisation and management of learning in a Personal Learning Environment?
- What kind of personal data should be shared and with whom to support learning achievements and personally successful learning?
- How can student's data privacy be guaranteed in PLEs, if it is to be connected to analytical tools applied for educational purposes?

Privacy Model in PLE

Several issues related to privacy in different types of PLEs are discussed in a first attempt to identify the relationship between privacy and PLEs and between privacy and students' learning control. For instance, informal Web 2.0 / Social Media PLEs, mobile PLEs, ePortfolio-based PLEs or badges-driven PLEs. As a result, a conceptual model of privacy in PLEs is developed to present current factors influencing on privacy. The model includes two levels of privacy control – learner-driven and institution-driven privacy control. Learner-driven privacy control is especially relevant in Web 2.0 / Social Media PLEs as well as in mobile PLEs, which are usually applied to support informal learning. Informal learning with PLEs gives more flexibility to learners to organise and control their private data. At the same time, learners in informal learning context are at a higher risk of disclose and misuse of private data. In contrast to that, institutional PLEs limit learners' possibility to control their privacy, but instead of that they protect learners from impropriate usage of their private data, e.g. by introducing certain regulations, such as Social Media Guidelines or keeping private data locked in an LMS. In the centre of the model, ePortfolio-based and badges-driven PLEs connect informal learning and formal learning contexts and require a both learners and institutions to apply common data privacy principles.

Conclusions and Future Work

The model summarizes the current situation of personal data usage in PLEs and could be used in the form of a recommendation tool explaining the possibilities for personal data sharing, organization and management and the influence of this fact on the data privacy. One of the key directions in emerging research may be the question of effective mechanisms for a responsible use and sharing of own and others private data in different media, learning systems, services and applications to enhance self-regulated learning in the context of growing diversity in Higher Education.

EFFECTIVE STRATEGIC DECISION MAKING ON OPEN AND DISTANCE EDUCATION ISSUES

Nikola Kadoić, Blaženka Divjak, Nina Begičević Ređep, University of Zagreb, Croatia

The research presented in this paper has been conducted in the scope of the project "Development of a methodological framework for strategic decision making in higher education – a case of open and distant learning implementation" (HigherDecision) supported by Croatian Science Foundation (web: higherdecision.foi.hr). The primary goal of HigherDecison project is to develop an overarching methodology for strategic decision making and monitoring of its implementation in HE.

In the first phase of our research, we have investigated which decision making (DM) methods and methodologies are used in the decision making processes in HE related to open and distance education (ODE). Results show the diversity of methods, methodologies and approaches used in the strategic decision making on ODE that proves complexity of the topic and variety of approaches. The most frequently used method is the Analytic Hierarchical Process (AHP) which is the most well-known multi-criteria decision making method (MCDM).

In the second phase of our research, we created a list of characteristics (demands) of DM methods in order to be applicable in the area of HE and ODE. We determined how different decision making methods fit those demands. Our conclusion is that the most suitable decision making method for strategic decision making in HE and ODE issues is the Analytical Network Process (ANP) because it enables modelling influences between elements (clusters and nodes) and most of DM problems in HE involve the interactions and dependences of higher-level elements in a hierarchy on lower-level elements. The ANP is a MCDM method introduced by Thomas Saaty as a generalization of the AHP method.

In the third phase of our research we listed the main ANP disadvantages and proposed the ANP upgrade that eliminates some of the identified disadvantages. Two main disadvantages of the ANP that we were focused on are a large number of comparisons that have to be made in decision making supported by the ANP and comparisons of clusters that are often very confusing and not understandable to decision makers (comparisons of two criteria/clusters with respect to the third one). Because of these disadvantages, the ANP is rarely used in practice. To deal with these disadvantages, we proposed an upgraded ANP method that combines the ANP with the Social Network Analysis (SNA). Both methods are based on graph theory that enables their combination. Basic elements of the SNA are nodes/vertices (elements) and ties/edges/loops (connections, ordered or unordered pairs of nodes). The ANP upgrades presented in our paper are based on the three main centrality measures and they were developed by using design science research process paradigm. In accordance with this approach, we have defined several types of ties for the purpose of upgrading the ANP. They are described and illustrated by practical example. Types of domination ties in upgraded method are as follows: (a) Domination ties are ties between nodes that come as a result of comparing criteria, alternatives and clusters by using so called Saaty's scale; (b) ties that describe influences between criteria; (c) influences between criteria resulted from alternatives as ties in network and (d) alternative domination ties. After identification of these ties and their weights, we use centrality measures to obtain weights of the criteria and priorities among alternative. In the original ANP method, we would have to compare clusters in pairs with respect to a goal. The clusters would also have to be compared with respect to other clusters depending on existence of ties between cluster criteria. In the upgraded ANP, we have to compare clusters only with respect to goals. Ties between clusters will be incorporated to clusters' weights with centrality measures.

With a new upgraded ANP, the number of criteria comparisons on cluster level is decreased and all comparisons that are result of criteria or cluster influences in original ANP are now excluded because influences are incorporated in the model through centrality measures. Further, decision makers do not have to do comparisons that usually are not understandable to them. Complexity of algorithm for finding solution of a decision making problem is also lowered. In the next phases of our research we are planning to do a validation of the developed method by using a number of simulations on different decision making problem structures.

ASSESSING DIVERSITY IN LEARNERS BACKGROUND AND PERFORMANCE

Anikó Balogh, László Pitlik, Ferenc Szani, Máté Schnellbach, Apertus Non-Profit Ltd., Hungary

Introduction

Assessing diversity in learners' background and performance assumes the observation of learning processes. Observation may be executed both in case of contact learning activities and especially in e-learning systems, where the storing of data logs is an essential part of system maintenance and system analysis. The observation of human individuals through questionnaires and/or interviews should always be interpreted on the basis of the parable of the "boiling frog". Storing logs apparently requires the definition of phenomena (being worth logging) in advance. It is – however – not the only method. Moreover, this method as such has inevitable risks. Lack of data in case of newer interpretation needs being generated in the hermeneutical process based on plan-oriented data. Instead of defining data needs in advance, it is possible to create logs which guarantee a high level of reproduction concerning each detail of the learning process. Reproduction-oriented logs always ensure the chance of being able to follow arbitrary analytical objectives any time. Therefore, the quality and efficiency of assessing diversity in learners' background and performance highly depends on the quality of data, where efficiency is considered as a kind of ratio between derived information added value and the resources needed. In this article, the authors focus on e-learning systems with high level reproduction capacity in the process of logging. Contact study activities are not examined at present, yet blended learning activities are also among the targeted features. The aim of this article is (based on real data assets over 10 millions of records) to outline an analytical system covering quasi 360° of analytical expectations for a decision support service using both classical statistics and artificial intelligence methods for modelling (e.g. robot teachers).

Discussion

Classic statistical analyses may lead to a kind of hermeneutical illusion with higher frequency than sophisticated models based on artificial intelligence approaches. Beside physical, physiological, cognitive illusions, hermeneutical illusions derive the wrong association based on hard facts and cellular intuition capacities like prejudice towards individuals, or bad estimations in the stock markets, etc. Statistical logic uses ratios to derive evaluations, but this sort of thinking can be instable. Infographics and their readers may both be diverse. The realization of a real graphical information added value is a kind of simulation problem. Based on the reader's attributes, the ideal parameters of infographics should be optimized. For the time being this is a task for visual artists. However, the concept of a robot designer may not be abandoned. Potential meanings of competence should be defined in such a clear way, that the change of competence may be measured automatically. Term-creation capability of artificial intelligence methods – like similarity analyses – ensures that words produced in the human brain can be transformed into source codes. The terms created should be compared to each other to see through the glass of term-creation possibilities, how consistent is the structure of facts. The reproduction level of learning processes is just a question of resources. Artificial intelligence based analyses make managing diverse terms possible in a numerical way. Model quality may be interpreted in new ways like consistency of models based on parallel function symmetry indices. Alternative solutions may be ranked following the logic of Occam's razor, where the parallel goodness criteria of the ideal solution are interpreted in case of each unique solution. Finally, a ranking model derives the best one, based on anti-discrimination principles. The basic goal within the field of info-graphics is the adaptation of the well-known visualization highlight from Hans Rosling. This solution can also be applied in the learning process as such, and in the interpretation processes of decision making/preparing. Time-orientation makes it possible to calculate economic impacts during the learning processes. Moreover, time is the navigation path for the interpretation of competence changes. Measurable phenomena can be stored in timestamp-driven tables. Changes between statuses are also a time dependent term. Therefore, time also delivers the basics for animations.

Summary

The main implications of the article are: log-quality should be optimized based on price/performance ratios for alternative reproduction levels including technical requirements and expected information added value. The human brain should deliver more and more terms as a specific output of the hermeneutical processes about e-learning behaviours, which may always be modelled by using artificial intelligence approaches. Decision support services may be generated in an adaptation procedure to exact decision needs.

AN ANALYSIS OF ICT POLICIES IN CANADA AND AUSTRALIA SECONDARY EDUCATION

Dorian Stoilescu, Western Sydney University, Australia

This paper discusses various similarities and differences in ICT curricula and policies between Canadian and Australian secondary education. While people see these two countries as having very similar cultural, social and educational backgrounds, the analysis of ICT curriculum shows major differences. After analysing the content and policies, it is believed that the Canadian ICT curriculum shows more programmatic approach to move computer science towards the next level: a) tertiary education instruction and b) mastering programming. Differently, Australian curriculum perceive ICT mostly from a learner sing technology, as a way of acquiring knowledge through the use of technology and less as a way of promoting programming and designing software. However, new trends show the Australian curriculum as being updated and important voices calling for more hours of programming in schools.

Summary

In the beginning of the 21st century, the impact of introducing information and communication technology (ICT) in society has been perceived by national and provincial governments as important paths of accelerating knowledge and economic growth. As such, ICT education became an important focus, as a way of speeding up the process of fostering ICT related knowledge and assure that future specialists are capable of continuing and improving the knowledge required in the advancement of technology. All world countries started important campaign of implementing ICT education in their national educational systems.

In particular, Canada and Australia have a great success in introducing ICT in all areas of society. Both countries are considered developed countries, have a common history as being part of Commonwealth, and have similar educational systems. These countries have large areas containing very diverse populations, from aboriginal or immigration roots. They have advanced technological level and a very sustainable internet infrastructure. The education is decentralized in both countries, as in Canada the provinces have the main responsibility of organizing the educational settings at all levels, while in Australia the states have similar reaching rights of organizing education similar to Canadian provinces. As well, both countries have experience in using standardized testing. For more than a decade, in both countries the ICT and Internet connectivity is almost universal. This paper will consider mostly ICT aspects from the New South Wales state from Australia and from Ontario province from Canada. This research has two main goals. First goal is to analyse the content of the ICT curricula in both countries and to show curricular similarities and differences between these two educational systems. Second goal, is to understand policies and the way ICT curricula is structured for the teachers and students.

THE SOCIAL DIMENSION OF EUROPEAN MOOC RESPONSE: MAKING DIVERSITY A STRENGTH!

Darco Jansen, EADTU – European Association of Distance Teaching Universities, the Netherlands

The MOOC hype in the media might be over, but investment and uptake of MOOCs are increasing significantly worldwide. By the end of 2015, approximately 6,850 courses were offered by 700+ universities to 58 million students. However, these figures exclude many European MOOC offering as mainly MOOC offering of the big (commercial) MOOC platforms listed. Many European universities have built an own platform or use a regional platform with a limited visibility. Most universities are not accepted by the big MOOC platforms in the US by lacking the reputation (in ranking) and finances to become a partner. As such, European efforts in MOOCs are less visible and divers. Consequently, also research data about MOOC participants, needs in society, etc. are strongly biased towards US dominance and lack evidence what really is going on in Europe. As many European MOOC efforts are local, there is a lack of coherent research at a European level. Only recently some efforts at European scale were conducted

For example, over 70% of European Higher Education Institutions (HEIs) do not support the idea that MOOCs should be paid for except for getting a formal credit as part of an accredited curriculum. I.e., there is strong support for the complete course for free to the participants. This is in contrast to recent changes of the big MOOC platform providers, tweaking their monetization model and shifting to pricing models where MOOCs are offered less for free or participants are tempted to take additional services for a fee. However, most European providers advocate that the full course, including some credit should be for free and as such MOOC provision must be financed by public means or private parties. In a recent European survey, the vast majority of their participants believed that MOOC support should mainly be financed by public means.

Moreover, MOOCs are becoming mainstream in Europe. Already four independent European studies show a strong MOOC involvement of HEIs. At least about 40% of HEIs in Europe are having MOOCs or planning to develop MOOCs soon against 12% in the US. However, in Europe the low or about zero penetration of MOOCs in the corporate world is somewhat surprising. Although some differences are observed between countries, it seems that a strong European involvement is widespread. These recent surveys also show that the uptake in Eastern Europe is catching up. In general, the strongest MOOC involvement of HEIs is seen in those regions with supportive policies and structures.

These results indicate a distinct European uptake of MOOCs related to different needs and to a different educational system compared to the US. The paper discusses the main results of various European studies and proposes various actions in making diverse European response a strength. This, amongst others include the important role of policy-makers and governments in the European context, the need for a European voice in a global MOOC market and how HEIs can increase their capacities in developing MOOCs.

THE GLOBAL MOOQ SURVEY: BUILDING A COMMON QUALITY REFERENCE FRAMEWORK FOR IMPROVING, ASSESSING AND COMPARING MOOC DESIGN

António Moreira Teixeira, Maria do Carmo Teixeira Pinto, Universidade Aberta, Portugal, Christian. M. Stracke, E. Tan, Open University of the Netherlands, Netherlands, Achiles Kameas, Bill Vassiliadis, Hellenic Open University, Greece, Gérard Vidal, École Normale Supérieur, France, Cleo Sgouropoulou, National Quality Infrastructure System, Greece

Societies and economies are experiencing a time of transition and change all over the world. As a consequence, Open (Online) Education has experienced a major development raising awareness amongst all actors. It has led to global grass-root movements, events, communities and associations as well as international policies and implementations in national and regional educational systems.

During the last years Massive Open Online Courses (MOOCs) became very popular, leading to an increasing debate about their quality as an education tool. To address the quality issues involved, the Massive Online Open Education Quality (MOOQ) project was initiated as the European Alliance for the Quality of MOOCs. It is a 3-year project funded by the European Union under the ERASMUS+ call. MOOQ is directly relevant to several key aspects of the 2011 EU Modernization Agenda.

The project's mission is to develop a quality reference framework for the adoption, the design, the delivery and the evaluation of MOOCs in order to empower MOOC providers for the benefit of the learners. The main goal of MOOQ is therefore the development and the integration of quality approaches, new pedagogies and organisational mechanisms into MOOCs with a strong focus on the learning processes, methodologies and assessments.

The first output of the MOOQ project is a global survey on existing practices and design patterns. The phenomena of MOOCs is a rather complex one as it results from different kind of approaches. This fact had important consequences in the diversity of formats used and also its features as well as the true nature and purpose of the educational experience they provide. In order to categorize design practices, MOOQ applied the typology suggested by Lisa Lane, based on the distinction between three basic categories: network-based, content-based and task-based MOOC models.

The development of the survey started with the establishment of a quality reference matrix comprising the basic categories of a typical MOOC design process. The research used as reference the process model of EN ISO/IEC 19796-1. This is based on the generic process model that is divided into seven process categories containing in total 38 processes. However, for the MOOQ objectives the first two categories were merged, giving way to only six process categories. The MOOQ quality reference process model consists therefore of three pillars which represent the main aspects involved in the production and delivery of MOOCs, each subdivided in 34 dimensions and respective descriptors.

As a consequence, a number of critical elements were identified and incorporated in the design of the surveys in order to allow for appropriate categorization of the design patterns. Three different surveys were prepared and launched, adjusting the 15 constructs to each of the target groups previously selected (learners, designers and facilitators). The surveys included each a mix of various types of items (open-end questions, five-level Likert questions, multiple-choice questions and yes/no questions) and are available in 3 different languages (English, French and Portuguese). An excess of 625 questionnaires (443 partially and 182 fully) were completed. An additional 36 semi-structured interviews with MOOC designers, facilitators and providers has been also carried out, allowing for complementarily of target groups addressed by each tool.

In this paper, the authors describe the research framework and the development process of the first global survey on MOOC design and explain how its results will inform a future common quality reference framework for improving, assessing and comparing MOOCs, which will itself lead to the development of a proposal for an international standard for MOOC design and delivery. At the EDEN conference, preliminary results of the surveys and semi-structured interviews conducted will be presented in detail.

THE IMPLICATIONS OF A NATIONAL HIGH-STAKES MOOC ON THE BUSINESS MODELS OF ACADEMIC INSTITUTIONS, AND ON THEIR FACULTY AND STUDENTS

Yoram M. Kalman, Ina Blau, The Open University of Israel, Israel

Technological innovation in higher education is actively discussed in the research literature and public discourse. Recently this discussion emphasizes the adoption of massive open online courses (MOOCs) and their potential impact on the business models of academic institutions, their faculty and students. Previous publications mostly explored low-stakes MOOCs that do not substitute traditional for-fee academic courses. This research of a high-stakes MOOC that substitutes an existing fee-based academic course, explores its impact on the institutional business model, faculty and students of academic institutions. The study is currently in its early stages. The lecture will present preliminary findings of the study.

Recently, a new high-stakes national MOOC sponsored by The Council for Higher Education, Israel's top academic authority, was launched. It focuses on reading comprehension of texts in academic English. Undergraduate students in Israel must demonstrate (through an exam) sufficient proficiency in academic English at some stage prior to graduation. Passing these exams is a significant hurdle for many students, especially for disadvantaged ones. Special units in each university and college offer students preparation courses in academic English. The fees for these courses are significant, and are additional to the regular undergraduate tuition costs. The MOOC "Academic English" offers participants access to extensive learning materials. These can be used as a self-paced MOOC meant to replace traditional Academic English courses, or as learning and practice materials to accompany and enrich traditional, campus-based Academic English courses through blended learning methods such as the "flipped classroom".

The launching of the Academic English MOOC led to an immediate significant drop in the number of students enrolling to the costly preparation courses offered by academic institutions. This led to a widespread controversy: Is the MOOC a proper alternative to the traditional courses? What about the instructors and academic units who were financially hurt by the decline in enrolments to the institutional (for-fee) courses?

The vast majority of MOOCs offered nowadays do not have a significant impact on the business model of higher education institutions since they cannot replace a "real" credit-bearing academic course. In contrast, in the case of this national Academic English MOOC, it is in direct competition with campus-based courses which are an important source of income for the institutions. These courses are also a significant financial and academic burden for the students. This is especially true for students with low levels of Academic English who are required to take several Academic English courses and are anxious to pass the proficiency tests that impede their academic progress. Thus, this course is high-stakes for both the students and the institutions.

The Academic English MOOC offers a unique opportunity to study the business model implications of a high-stakes MOOC that can substitute an existing fee-based academic course. Thus, the overarching research questions of this study are: (a) How does the Academic English MOOC influence the business models of the Academic English units in different Israeli higher education institutions, their faculty and students? (b) How do these business models in turn influence the adoption, use and diffusion of the MOOC among Academic English teachers and learners?

The business model of the unit in charge of teaching academic English in five to seven different higher education institutions will be explored. Semi-structured interviews were conducted with 10 leaders and decision makers at these Academic English units, with the goal of describing each unit's customer value proposition, infrastructure (resources and processes), and financial model.

The business model and the role of the Academic English MOOC in teaching and learning will be further elaborated based on semi-structured interviews with 10 English instructors at each unit, as well as with 10 students in the traditional classes and 10 students in the Academic English MOOC. Such triangulation of data from different sources strengthens the validity of the findings and enables comprehensive examination of the phenomenon. The inclusion in the study of students from both categories enables exploring the differences between students who are exposed to the MOOC in the form of technology-enhanced learning materials incorporated in traditional courses and students who have chosen a self-pathed learning of the Academic English MOOC.

FACTORS THAT PREDICT DIFFERENTIAL ONLINE VERSUS FACE-TO-FACE COURSE OUTCOMES: EVIDENCE FROM GERMANY AND THE UNITED STATES

Claire W. Wladis, Borough of Manhattan Community College and the Graduate Center – City University of New York, Alyse C. Hachey, Katherine M. Conway, Borough of Manhattan Community College – City University of New York, United States of America

Online Learning and Higher Education in the United States and Germany

The U.S. and German education systems both have a recent history of rapid enrolment expansion and struggle with upward educational mobility in comparison to international averages.

Both the U.S. and Germany have an education structure that is organized primarily at the state level but German system's early tracking results in proportionately fewer students obtaining a tertiary educational credential.

Online education, which is rapidly expanding worldwide, may provide increased access and research suggests similar learning outcomes are achieved, but attrition in online classes is higher than in traditional face to face classes. This study explores the interaction between the online medium and student characteristics in predicting subsequent course outcomes. Specifically, we ask:

- Which student characteristics exacerbate or mitigate differences in rates of online versus face-to-face course retention and successful course completion?
- Which characteristics make students more likely to drop-out of college after taking an online course?
- To what extent do online course outcomes explain subsequent college dropout?

If online courses have lower completion rates, they may hinder degree completion. It is therefore essential to identify which students are at highest risk of failing or dropping out of those courses if they enrol in them online, so that interventions can be targeted to those students at highest risk.

Methodology and Results

This study uses data from the 2014-2015 fall/winter semester: from the 18 two- and four-year colleges in the City University of New York (CUNY) system in the U.S.; and from 30 colleges and universities in the German province of Bavaria. At the end of the semester, students were invited to participate in an online survey. Outcomes in online versus face-to-face courses taken by the same student were compared; propensity score matching and multi-level models were also used to control for differences in student characteristics.

This research looked at three outcomes: course success, course failure and college persistence. The main independent variable (IV), course medium, was dichotomized to face-to-face or fully online, and covariates included a wide range of student characteristics.

The results varied by country. Native born students in the U.S. are at greater risk of online drop-out, whereas the reverse is true in Germany. Being the parent of a young child was also a risk factor in the U.S. but not in Germany. In both countries, higher course/credit loads contributed to increased drop out, as did lower grade point averages.

Policy and Practice Implications

Colleges wanting to target interventions to students at highest risk in the online environment may want to focus on students with lower grade point averages, student parents (in countries with less state support for parents of young children), and students who are enrolled in higher numbers of courses/credits. Whether native-born or foreign-born students are in need of targeted interventions depends on the national/cultural context, and more research is needed to understand how other factors explain the relationship between nationality and online outcomes.

APPLICATION OF SOCIAL NETWORKING AS A REFLECTIVE LEARNING AND CRITICAL THINKING TOOL

Les Pang, University of Maryland University College, United States of America

The presentation examines the use of Twitter, a social networking tool, in a graduate level online class to support reflective learning and critical thinking. It describes a study in which students participated in a weekly learning activity in which they would share their reflections from the course through the use of Twitter messages and demonstrate critical thinking. A survey was conducted to capture student reactions to the use of this social networking media for these purposes.

EFFECTIVE LEARNING THE PROPEL-LEARN WAY: AN EVIDENCE BASED, MOBILE DELIVERED PROGRAM ENGENDERING SELF-DIRECTED LIFE LONG LEARNING HABITS AND STRATEGIES FOR DISTANCE EDUCATION STUDENTS AND STAFF

Ignatius G.P. Gous, University of South Africa, South Africa

The Reality – too much to know

Learners need to have the ability to master masses of information in short times. They also need to be able to discern, evaluate and weigh information as to its quality and reliability, while at the same time mastering the ability to change information into useable knowledge to grapple with relevant issues. The realities are, however, that teaching often still is archaic in the sense that it mainly focuses on the mere mastery of facts, which is necessary, but not sufficient to address the realities of our times. Where there are attempts to transform teaching, it is sometimes based on pop psychology and neuro-myths, and might do more harm than good. It is also true that there is solid research available about minds, brain and education, but often these research results are hidden from practical application in the real life situations where it is needed. The question is, however, when has education reached its goal? For a very long time education focussed on the content of the discipline or subject that is being taught, and assessment centred around testing whether the content has been mastered. Currently, however, we are faced with an information overload as never before. For this reason, the focus is shifting towards also developing learning skills in humans. This is seen as of particular interest to students at Distance Education institutions, and especially to people in the workplace after completion of their formal studies which continues to the end of their careers and even thereafter. Equally, often learners are being coached to pass school, instead of being taught how to learn and master the necessary skills and knowledge in the field they are working in. To address this in the long term, education and training needs to be carried out more efficiently. In the short term, current learners and also employees need to be continuously up-skilled and re-skilled, coupled with developing the ability of life-long learning. There is a myriad of study method programs available, varying substantially in terms of effectiveness, validity and groundedness in reputable research. Many are based on what can be called neuromyths, which are ideas claiming to have a solid foundation in neuro- and cognitive science research, but which are devoid of any scientific basis. Similarly, often people rely on "Study Method Courses", hoping that mastering a few "tricks and trades" of studying will be sufficient.

The Proposal – a workable program

What is rather needed is a comprehensive human development program that aims to instil positive traits and habits in a person, linked to meaningful life goals. A truly effective approach should therefore address realities such as Identity, Mastery and Legacy.

- Addressing the *Identity* of the learner, attention is given to self-knowledge, determination as well as the ability to focus.
- Attending to *Mastery*, the skills of Listening, Reading (on paper and on screen), Studying and Memory are shared.
- Striving for leaving a worthwhile *Legacy*, the ability to Perform and show what you know, as well as to apply and create is taught and coached.

It is more than a "study method course", in the sense that it aims to assist student in launching habits for a life-long journey of self-directed learning. The program is made available as web based lessons, which can be accessed from any mobile or computer device with access to the internet. It is aimed at being light on data, making useable for even for students in developing countries with older feature phones. The program is available in English, Afrikaans, Russian, and Chinese, with translations in more languages to be added soon.

More information about the program is available at cerebration.info or on http.//cerebration.teachable.com.

DIVERSITY AND DIGITALIZATION AS VITAL KEY SUCCESS FACTORS FOR INDIVIDUALISATION OF LEARNING

Helge Gerischer, Anne Götze, Eric Forkel, Julia Kauper, Christian-Andreas Schumann, Kevin Reuther, Claudia Tittmann, West Saxon University of Zwickau, Germany

Digital transformation as driver of the epochal change

Transformation means conversion, re-modelling, re-designs as well as changes and revisions. The peculiarity of the present epoch is that omnipresent transformations are superimposed by omnipresent digitization. If both are connected to one another, then the key driver is called digital transformation. Transformations lead to a drive to rationalize with the help of digital technologies and media, which in turn lead to further transformations.

Holistic development of organisations

The holistic business process management is an important component of sustainable success recipes for organizations. The business process design is required when new business fields have to be integrated into existing process landscapes or new technical possibilities are introduced. Diversification leads to new business areas, digitization extends the technical possibilities. For this reason, organisations under the pressure of digital transformations have to go through this design process in several iterations.

Relevance of diversity as organisational principle

Diversity is an organisational principle. It is part of any organisational development, especially of its strategic orientation. Diversity influences all basic strategies. Diversification strategy is a sophisticated approach for vertical extension of organisational activities such as new products in the same application field or new technologies for the available products or vertical expansion of organisational activities such as new offers of upstream or downstream services in relation to the organisational core processes.

Relevance of digitalization as organisational principle

Many processes of any nature in the society are automated or part automated with the support of information technologies. Thereby, they are automatically transferred into a digitized world. In general, the digital transformation influences the development of organisation by four levers: digital data, automation, interconnection and human-machine-transactions. The digitalisation is precondition and part of the digital transformation.

Inter-organisational relation of diversity and digitalisation

The inter-organisational context of diversity and digital systems was already given by the traditional information and technology management. The business continuity management based on the contingency planning including emergency plan, vital record plan, and backup plan supported by means of some combination of redundancy, diversity, mobility. Therefore, diversity is one of the key aspects for the development of organisational and of inter-organisational strategy and structure.

Impact of diversity and digitalisation on individualisation of learning

Diversification and globalization are inextricably linked. The trend is being reinforced by digitalization. Learners become more mobile through digital techniques and digital products. They are better and better able to choose from the wide range of offers, those which best appropriate to their interest. Educational organisations must adapt their strategies to the changes in time. The interaction of users in social networks accelerates this process enormously. The stronger individualisation is based on a comprehensive diversification in connection with the digitisation.

Individualisation of learning in practice

The prerequisite for the individualisation of learning is the design of modular learning systems. Once developed learning components have to be used as often as possible because otherwise the efficiency of the learning offers is usually not guaranteed. The development of individual learning modules from a basic and well-structured knowledge is technically, organisationally, contently, socially and economically feasible. These smallest knowledge modules can be mapped in semantic networks in order to make them available for individual learning paths.

Individualisation as part of mass consumption in learning and training

Individualisation becomes part of the mass consumption in learning and training. It is the complementary development to the mass component production for user-individualised products in industry. After structuring the contents, the semantic network has been developed for creating an individual, on-demand generation of courses.

Conclusions

The mainstreams in the society are recently characterized by digital transformations. The result is an epochal and global change. The further successful development of organizations depends on the holistic understanding, design and control of the systems in general and of the educational systems in particular. Diversity is not only a characteristic of a system or its processes and function as well as products and services, but it becomes more and more an organisational principle. The same development is typical for the digitalisation. It will lead to more changes in the end, the so-called digital transformations of the educational systems.

WRITING TO LEARN WITH AUTOMATED FEEDBACK THROUGH (LSA) LATENT SEMANTIC ANALYSIS: EXPERIENCES DEALING WITH DIVERSITY IN LARGE ONLINE COURSES

Miguel Santamaría Lancho, Mauro Hernández, Jose Maria Luzón Encabo, Guillermo Jorge-Botana, UNED, Spain

The increasing demand for higher education and life-long training has induced a raising supply of online courses provided both by distance education institutions and conventional face to face universities. Simultaneously, public universities' budgets have been experiencing serious cuts, at least in Europe. Due to this shortage of human and material resources, large online courses usually face great challenges to provide an extremely diverse student community with quality formative assessment, specially, the kind that offers rich and personalized feedback. Peer to peer assessment could partially address the problem, but involves its own shortcomings.

Writing to learn (WTL) is a way to foster critical thinking and a suitable method to train soft skills such as analysis and synthesis abilities. These skills are the base for other complex learning methodologies such as PBL, case method, etc. WTL approach requires a regular feedback given by dedicated lecturers.

Consistent assessing of free-text answers is more difficult than we usually assume, specially, when addressing large or massive courses. Using multiple choice "objective" assessment appears an obvious alternative. However, the authors feel that this alternative shows serious shortcomings when aiming to produce outcomes based on written expression and complex analysis.

To face this dilemma, the authors decided to test an LSA-based automatic assessment tool developed by researchers of Developmental and Educational Psychology Department at UNED (Spanish National Distance Education University) named G-Rubric. The experience was launched in 2014-2015. By using GRubric, we provided automated formative and iterative feedback to our students for their open-ended (70-200 words).

Some conclusions can be drawn from our experience:

- Automated-assessment software such as Gallito-G-Rubric is currently mature enough to be used with students obtaining quite satisfactory results in terms of acceptable accuracy.
- This kind of systems is particularly apt and useful for on-line teaching, especially in massive courses such as MOOC. Nevertheless, they show also great potential for face-to-face or mixed teaching at any level.
- The experience of adapting such a system to assess free-text short-answer questions to Economic History proved reasonably affordable in terms of time and effort invested.

The trial's results seem to point out that interacting with G-Rubric can improve learning by giving detailed feedback: (a) encourages devoting more time to the task; (b) increases 'earnings' in the quality of answers; (c) increases motivation to work on activities (d) helps students to achieve better final answers. In this sense, it may soon become a viable tool for formative assessment. In the near future, automated assessment systems will be part of the teacher's toolbox, as Virtual Learning Environments are today. LSA-based systems such as G-Rubric are a solid candidate to a leading role in that process.

BLENDED LEARNING TO SUPPORT A DIVERSE GRADUATE COHORT DURING CAMPUS DISRUPTIONS: BARRIER OR BLESSING?

Ingrid le Roux, Lynette Nagel, University of Pretoria, South Africa

Introduction

A new approach to graduate studies at a contact University was necessary with blended learning as a potential vehicle to achieve program continuity. The University propagated the use of technology to counter the disruptions brought on by student unrest, and provide quality tuition. What was not known is how ready the graduate students in an entrepreneurship course were for their Masters' studies, or the blended and flipped learning approach that was implemented in 2016. Students had diverse linguistic, cultural and previous academic backgrounds. Most were working full-time and faced challenges related to balancing work/family and study roles, therefore coaching conversations were conducted to provide study and social support.

The focus of this study was to observe the perceived preparedness of graduate students in a coursework module for their degree program, and their experience of a blended teaching method. Research questions addressed the following:

- What barriers do entrepreneurship students experience when starting their Masters' studies?
- How does a blended environment influence their ability to overcome such barriers?

Methodology

Considering the small group of very diverse students, qualitative analysis of student narratives and interviews were compared with their responses to a questionnaire that probed their concerns at the start of the course. Their access, skills and use of technology for learning was important to cope with a flipped teaching approach. Known challenges in post-graduate studies were also probed, including academic writing skills, conducting research, motivation and time management.

Findings

Contrary to expectations, these students were not severely hampered by technology or computer skills, having enough confidence to use the University web infrastructure, and had high levels of motivation. They were less sure of research, particularly academic writing and –resources, probably due to diverse previous studies. Those who fell behind from the start had a serious drawback that could not be overcome. Required written peer review uncovered lack of confidence in some students. Everybody preferred watching videos on the theory to attending lectures. A scaffolded approach to analysing articles was effective and also enabled them to make meaningful contributions to group assignments. Group collaborative assignments and self-regulated group activities were well received and executed. All students attended individual coaching interviews and reported the benefits thereof towards organising their studies and lives better, which contributed to academic success.

Conclusions

Students were initially particularly worried about their academic writing skills and their ability to juggle their time between studies, work and other responsibilities. The online environment was perceived as clear and structured. Students experienced online collaborative activities very positively due to convenient online meeting times, that helped them manage their time, one of their biggest concerns. The value of the coaching conversations turned most of their personal and learning barriers around, helped them to manage their time and priorities, and contributed towards successful course completion. Both the insights from the coaching conversation and the online learning skills contributed to the development of self-regulated, independent learners. We recommend that a structured, scaffolded introduction to research methodology and academic writing from the very beginning will dispel many doubts. In addition to resources supporting online activity, recognition should be given to students' personal and emotional stresses and needs for which capable facilitation or coaching is indispensable. It is clear that in diverse student cohorts, unique barriers and concerns should be anticipated and addressed.

ICT PROFESSIONAL DEVELOPMENT BY ENCOURAGING COMMUNITIES AND NETWORKS ACROSS FIVE CLOSELY LOCATED K12 SCHOOLS

Stefan Hrastinski, Marianne Ekman, KTH Royal Institute of Technology, Sweden

Many studies have found that participation in teacher communities is an essential part of professional development. Such professional development could be described as a relational-responsive approach to change because thoughts and activities emerge inside relationships rather than outside or planned beforehand. Most research has focused on teacher communities within schools. One of the weaknesses of the community perspective is that each community creates epistemic barriers between different communities. For example, a mathematics teacher community and physical education teacher community might describe and understand their use of ICT in different ways, although they share a common interest, i.e. to improve learning. Thus, a key challenge is to coordinate the knowledge produced in different communities. Individuals and communities can be connected through networks, inside and across schools. The aim of this paper is to explore how the encouragement of communities and networks could contribute to ICT professional development across schools. This paper is based on a project, carried out during 2013-2015, with the purpose to encourage ICT professional development across five Swedish K12 schools. These schools are located in a quite small geographical area, within walking distance from each other, and all activities and meetings for the teachers were conducted at these schools. The authors of this paper participated as action researchers, and encouraged the formation of a school leader community and lead teacher community. The school leader community included two or three school leaders from each school and the lead teacher community included one or two lead teachers from each school. The lead teachers mainly worked as teachers but were also expected to support and encourage ICT professional development. They organized conferences and workshops, inspired by the TeachMeet model, and complemented with opportunities for reflection for the teachers in the five schools. There were about 230 teachers working in the five schools, representing all grades and subject disciplines. All seven participants of the lead teacher community were interviewed. Each semi-structured interview was about one hour and was subsequently recorded and transcribed. The lead teacher community played a central role, but ICT professional development was dependent on the interplay of different types of communities and networks. We identified six examples of communities and networks: (a) *School leader community:* A community with the shared common purpose to make joint decisions that were necessary in order to enable ICT professional development across the five schools; (b) *Online teacher network:* The lead teachers primarily gained inspiration by following other teachers by using social media; (c) *Lead teacher community:* A community with the shared common purpose of organizing large-scale professional development in conferences and workshops; (d) *Teacher network:* The teachers of the five schools were loosely connected in a network with the common purpose of sharing experience of using ICT in pedagogical practice; (e) *Intra-school teacher community:* Some teachers worked in intra-school teacher communities with the common purpose of improving their use of ICT in pedagogical practice, based on what was learnt during the conferences and workshops; (f) *Inter-school teacher network:* Teachers belonging to smaller subject disciplines, such as home economics and physical education, jointly formed inter-school networks with the common purpose of sharing experience of using ICT in subject-specific pedagogical practice. The study illustrates that ICT professional development across the five schools was dependent on different types of communities and networks. It was evident that the organization of joint activities also contributed to learning in unexpected ways, such as spontaneously initiated intra-school teacher communities and inter-school teacher networks. Examples of challenging and developing the use of ICT in pedagogical practice were mainly identified in the intra-school teacher communities. These were spontaneously formed and used the teacher networks as inspiration and influx of ideas, which were then adapted and implemented by teachers in their specific settings. It can be expected that other school-school collaboration projects would also be characterized by a complex interplay of communities and networks. School leaders, lead teachers, and others that initiate ICT professional development across schools, need to be aware that they are essential in encouraging structures and cultures that support the development of communities and networks. These communities and networks will live a life of their own and will contribute to ICT professional development in unforeseen ways.

FRAMEWORK FOR DIGITALLY MATURE SCHOOLS

Nina Begičević Ređep, Igor Balaban, Bojan Žugec, Marina Klačmer Čalopa, Blaženka Divjak,
University of Zagreb, Croatia

Introduction

Rapid diffusion of Information and Communication Technologies (ICT) in all professional and personal areas require digital maturity from schools. In order to assess this aspect of school, a concept of digitally mature school has been developed and translated into different frameworks. In this paper, we describe development methodology of Framework for Digitally Mature Schools (FDMS) in Croatia. The FDMS, together with the accompanying instrument and software, represents a comprehensive tool set for the assessment of digital maturity of a school. The FDMS recognized 5 areas divided into 38 elements that are described on five digital maturity levels in the form of a rubric. It was being developed within the framework of e-Schools project (http://www.carnet.hr/e-skole) by Faculty of Organization and Informatics, University of Zagreb and CARNet (Croatian Academic and Research Network).

Objectives of the research

The overall objectives of the research related to the FDMS are:

- to review the existing findings on maturity of schools, to propose main areas and elements, to describe digital maturity of schools and to build a comprehensive framework for digitally mature schools;
- to develop the Instrument (in form of a rubric and accompanying questionnaire) for self-evaluation and external evaluation of schools in order to be able to determine the digital maturity level for each school;
- to assess the level of digital maturity of schools in Croatia by using the developed Instrument;
- to perform in-depth analysis of maturity levels of all schools included in the research, as well as to monitor their progress and plan the means of support within e-Schools project.

Research methodology

The methodological approach we used for the development of the FDMS was for the most part qualitative. In the first phase, we have done a comprehensive qualitative analysis of 15 frameworks for the digital maturity. In the second phase, we applied sorting cards method and two focus groups analysis as tools for defining new framework areas and their elements as well as descriptors related to the levels. In the third phase, the experts who developed the framework now determined the descriptors for all levels in rubrics form (questionnaire on 70 examinees). The fourth phase resulted with the rubric for each domain with 5 maturity levels, 5 areas and 38 elements. We used mathematical logic with logical operations and quantifiers to clearly connect statements and accurately describe maturity levels. In the fifth development phase, there were several consecutive iterations of improving the Framework and descriptor elements with help of experts. Developed FDMS consists of five areas and five levels of digital maturity of schools. The main five areas of the digital maturity within the FDMS are: (a) Planning, management and leadership, (b) ICT in learning and teaching, (c) Development of digital competences, (d) ICT culture and (e) ICT infrastructure. Each area consists of a larger number of elements which have been described for each maturity level: Basic, Initial, e-Enabled, e-Confident and e-Mature.

Conclusion

The FDMS, the Instrument for evaluation of the digitally mature schools and the supporting software represent a unique and comprehensive tool set created according to sound research methodology. Due to their generic characteristics, the FDMS and the Instrument can be applied in other educational systems and countries with minor adjustments. The Instrument can be used as a tool to evaluate the school's digital maturity level but also for the identification of the areas for improvement that could enable the growth on the scale of digital maturity and improve the overall reputation and school results. The FDMS, the Instrument and the accompanying software have been already successfully applied in the process of self-evaluation and external evaluation of 151 schools in Croatia. The significant feedback for improvement of the FDMS and of the Instrument was collected in this validation process. The evaluation of further 1400 elementary and high-schools in Croatia is planned for 2017.

DBS (DATA BACKGROUND SEARCH) MODEL TO SUPPORT CHILD PROTECTION PRACTICES IN INDIA

Shubham Kumar, KIIT University, India, William Rivera Hernández, Laurea University of Applied Sciences, Finland, Kokshetau State University, Republic of Kazakhstan

Aim

Renovating the conventional education system by: (a) developing a verification system to check for serial offenders of crimes against children with special emphasis on education sector, for selecting professionals who are free from any stain stemming from either conviction or accusation; (b) training professionals dealing with children in child protection practices and inclusion of diversity in broader sense of term (from gender, social-cultural background, differently able pupils and religion).

Methodology

We used an ethnography approach to assess the current status of education and wellbeing and Child Friendly School experiences of children in rural India. Various set of activities were carried out with the children during which active observation was adopted in order to detect perceived and actual vulnerabilities, as well as child's involvement in the activities. The collected data was contrasted with current legal framework by interviewing an expert lawyer.

The interview was also done to ascertain the present provision for child protection and its implementation. To this extend the lack of a centralized search facility comparable to the UK DBS system is perceived as a major impediment for India to develop a proper scrutiny approach in the recruitment of teaching staff.

Work carried out

A random sample of children was selected by inviting them to participate freely in the drawing and playing activities. The facilitator introduced the aim of the session and told the children that we wanted to hear and learned about their school's experiences.

It was observed by our legal expert that the success of conviction in child abuse cases depends upon the efficient investigation of the offence and quick collection of the incriminating evidences. It is not in dispute that there is a provision for the special courts in both the circumstances but the courts have its own limitations. Unless and until some palpable and concrete evidence is brought on the record the courts cannot convict an offender. It has been found that very often false cases are being filed in the special provisions to take revenge from the persons. Thus, good investigation and keeping a proper record of evidence data would efficiently eliminate the misuse of these laws.

Conclusion

After analysing the collected data and introspection of the Legal framework and its loopholes, it is hence concluded that there is a compelling need of a central database of Convicts of Child Abuse (Physical and Sexual). It could help the government keep a tab on regular offender to try to slip into jobs of teaching/day care to commit these horrendous crimes. This database (DBS) would ensure that a convict/accused of a serious crime against children is monitored irrespective of the state or city he lives in or in many cases, tries to relocate. It would be also helpful in catching and inspecting serial offenders who under the present rules, easily relocated and hide from the authorities. This would be beneficial for the combined recruitment drive of teachers in public schools as DBS can be used as a verification system to scrutinize the candidates.

Moreover, a module could be designed for the teachers which could help in dealing with children in child protection practices and inclusion of diversity in broader sense of term (from gender, social-cultural background, differently able pupils and religion). In this way the teachers would be more equipped in handling diversity related issues in Education precinct.

PLEKHANOV RUSSIAN UNIVERSITY OF ECONOMICS: THE EXPERIENCE OF LIFELONG EDUCATION IMPLEMENTING

Olga A. Grishina, Dinara R. Tutaeva, Alexey I. Grishin,
Plekhanov Russian University of Economics, Russian Federation

Lifelong education indeed has its place deserved among key components of sustainable and effective development of human capital, as well as increase of competitive capabilities of University graduates at the labour market. In the Plekhanov RUE almost all levels of education currently available in the Russian Federation are implemented – secondary general education, secondary vocational education, higher education, including postgraduate and doctoral studies, additional education. The University provides all necessary conditions for acquiring the basic and additional qualifications not only during the period of study at the University but also throughout the whole employment period and lifetime in general. The key role in this system is played by the Faculty of Distance Learning (FDL), which covers almost all aspects of lifelong education provided for different group of learners – from freshmen-students to graduates of the Plekhanov, and from 1st year schoolchildren to senior citizens.

For children – the "University Saturdays" project

The "University Saturdays" is an educational career guidance project for school and college students implemented since 2014 and held under the support of the Moscow Department of Education. Within the bounds of this project a range of activities were organized by the FDL of the Plekhanov RUE in cooperation with other faculties and departments aimed at attracting students to the University. For years of 2014-2016, 3595 schoolchildren and college students had participated in the project. Among all project educational activities, there are master classes, trainings, quests, lectures and excursions focused on such topics as history, social science, basics of economics and accounting, art etc. Together with schoolchildren and college students attend events with their parents and teachers have participated in the majority of the events outlined above, remarking the high level of them.

For students and adults – FDL opens its doors!

Nowadays 41 basic educational programs are implemented at the Plekhanov RUE Faculty of Distance learning for more than 4000 listeners, and a number of additional professional programs for about 1000 students. Thus, upon graduation students may receive not only the higher education diploma, but also acquire additional competences and the right to conduct a new type of professional activity. According to the graduates, a record in the summary about an additional education gives them preferences in employment. Students of the Plekhanov University (as well as other Universities) are also offered with a wide portfolio of additional educational programs developed in conjunction with employers. Among the most interesting and popular projects of the FDL was the one carried out in close cooperation with the OBI retail company from December 2015 to July 2016, as a result of which the professional training program 'Universal head of store department' for the last-year PRUE students was developed. The program was completely free for students, being funding by the sponsor (OBI, which was also the customer of the research project). Classes were conducted by PRUE teachers and employees of OBI, at both PRUE campus and the company head office. After completion of the program, students received a diploma on professional retraining, and the best of them were employed in the company.

For seniors – "Silver Generation University" project and more

The older generation is not to remain without attention of the Plekhanov University. In 2014, the FDL co-organized the IV All-Russian Championship on computer decathlon among pensioners conducted by the Russian Union of Pensioners, in which 130 pensioners – winners of regional competitions from Russia, Belgium, Slovakia and Belarus participated. This Championship has not only become an annual event in the PRUE, but also has led to the launch of the FDL social project for seniors called 'Silver Generation University'. Within the bounds of it a number of activities are conducted, such as creative weeks and master classes aimed to increase consumer, computer and legal literacy of the older people, excursions and lectures devoted to such topics as history and art, etc. 'Silver Generation University' has more than 300 listeners now and continue developing.

E-LEARNING AND MULTICULTURALITY IN MEXICO

Edith Tapia-Rangel, Jorge León-Martínez, National Autonomous University of Mexico, Mexico

Cultural Diversity

If culture includes arts and letters, as well as ways of life, value systems, traditions and beliefs, then cultural diversity is "the multiplicity of ways in which the cultures of societies are expressed; when it manifests it, enriches and transmits the cultural heritage of humanity through diverse modes of artistic creation, production, dissemination, distribution and enjoyment by the various generations that inhabit the planet". As a member of UNESCO, Mexico endorsed both the 2001 Universal Declaration on Cultural Diversity and the 2005 Convention on the Protection and Promotion of the Diversity of Cultural Expressions. Taking into account this national context, in 2004 the National Autonomous University of Mexico (UNAM) created the University Program: Mexico, as a Multicultural Nation (PUMNM). This program was absorbed in 2014 by the University Program of Studies of Cultural Diversity and Interculturality (PUIC).

This program has generated various strategies to achieve its purpose, such as: Research lines delimiting projects; Research programs that deal interculturality themes; Academic projects that serve different areas; Scholarship system for indigenous students; Diplomates to strengthen the leadership of indigenous women, Elective course: Mexico, Multicultural Nation.

Elective Course: Mexico, Multicultural Nation

This subject is taught in 12 schools or faculties of UNAM, and it is an optional course in three more faculties. In 2015, 1,709 students attended this course. For students, this course has been attractive for students because of among other things for the transversality of the subject in the different schools, the interdisciplinary, and the advantage of being able to attend the classes in different schools. In this way, it's also possible to integrate students into wide student university networks. It is also important to mention that the subject has been highly recommended among them. In 2012, the Coordination of Open University and Distance Education (CUAED) was requested to generate the online course "Mexico, Multicultural Nation" in September 2014, this course. Some of the topics included in this subjects are: Mexico, Multicultural Nation; The indigenous People and Communities; Our Third Root; The Mexicans who gave us the world; The State of Development of the Indigenous People; The Environment and the Indigenous People; The Indigenous Rights; The Indigenous Women; Migration; The Indigenous Education; Health and Medicine among the Indigenous People; The Indigenous Literature; Interethnic Relations and Multiculturalism; and so on.

Each course has the following structure:

Unit Structure	Theme Structure
Introduction, General objective, Theme, Way of working (Support materials, Media), Way of working, Calendar and Accreditation criteria	Introduction, Specific objective, Content, Glossary, Learning Activity (optional), Self-assessment (optional), Opinion survey (optional), Reference sources

Conclusions

The respect and promotion of cultural diversity is an action that UNESCO seeks to promote in all its member countries. In the case of Mexico, laws have been adopted and programs are implemented to achieve this. Specifically, in the UNAM it has been created the University Program for the Study of Cultural Diversity and Interculturalism to form, investigate and disseminate issues related to Multiculturalism. As part of its training strategy, it was created the transversal subject "Mexico, Multicultural Nation" that can be integrated in the curricular map of its different degrees, seeking to expand the offer by putting it online with the support from CUAED. The path has been designed to fulfil the commitment of a nation that respects multiculturalism, preserves its wealth and promotes harmony among its members.

ALTERNATIVE EDUCATION IS THE BEST POLICY FOR THE FUTURE

Areej Alsaysi, Taibah University, Saudi Arabia

This study investigates the need to develop alternative education programs in Saudi Arabia and indicate the most suitable ones for the Saudi context. The study has adopted a qualitative methodology and incorporates interviews with faculty members at the Faculty of Education in Taibah University (Madinah, Saudi Arabia). The results gleaned from the study reveal that all study participants agree a on the real need for alternative education programs in Saudi Arabia. However, some participants expressed concerns about the suitability of the Saudi context for such programs. The interviewees have also indicated their eagerness to see such programs implemented in the country as they would provide an excellent environment that meets student needs. Accordingly, the current study puts forward a demand for educationalists and relevant decision makers in Saudi Arabia to allow for this critical improvement in the country's education system through the smooth integration of alternative education programs.

EVALUATING THE RESULTS OF USING OERS, PERS, BLENDING AND FLIPPING TO DELIVER A COMPUTER SYSTEMS MODULE TO YEAR 1 STUDENTS

Michael O'Rourke, Athlone Institute of Technology, Ireland

The key aim of this project is to incentivise higher education students to engage with a Year 1 Computer Systems module through a blended and flipped classroom approach. Attendance at the traditional lecture is in decline for a variety of reasons. The concept for this module is to encourage self-directed learning (SDL) through reading Proprietary Educational Resource (PER) material and watching Open Educational Resource (OER) video in advance of class assessments. The actual class time is used for discussion of the content of lessons using PowerPoint summaries, watching related videos, online assessment and laboratory work. The project aims to measure and evaluate the effectiveness of this approach. The results of this project are examined and discussed, after a one-year implementation, by means of a survey of these students.

REOPEN – RECOGNITION OF VALID AND OPEN LEARNING

Airina Volungevičienė, Vytautas Magnus University, Lithuania, Ferenc Tátrai, EDEN, United Kingdom, Vida Žvinienė, Marius Šadauskas, Vytautas Magnus University, Lithuania

Introduction

Opening Up education – apart from the need for structural changes – also created challenges and opportunities in curriculum opening up represented by

- Open Educational Resources and MOOCs;
- open collaboration and communication among teachers and learners;
- creating innovative education services for diverse learning groups and
- recognition and validation of non-formal open learning.

The ReOpen project follows recommendations stated in the EC JRC research study on "Validation of Non-formal MOOC-based learning" (2016) by establishing validated open learning practices: there is a need for

- validated Open Online Learning (OOL) curriculum examples;
- digitally smart learning environments leading to OOL recognition and
- case scenarios on recognition of validated non-formal open learning.

Scope

The project addresses the objectives of the "Opening Up" initiative and implements the recommendations of the EC JRC Case study by

- establishing validated open learning practices;
- offering learner credentials for online and open learning (OOL) by verification of learner identity, setting learning agreement and other instruments;
- establishing digital badges for recognition of learning achievements;
- establishing collaboration with institutions to provide transparent information on potential recognition of OOL;
- providing teacher training with the tools for OOL development and recognition.

Expected results

The project creates an online platform for non-formal open learning curriculum development with learning validation and recognition instruments in place (learner credentials, digital badges, learning path recognition and assessment tools), and prepares training materials for teachers and trainers in (C-)VET, HE, companies and adult learning organisations on

- designing non-formal open learning curriculum;
- application of digital badges for credentialing the learning achievements;
- recognition of non-formal open learning in formal curricula.

Based on the above, a short term joint staff training event will be held using the above training materials and 5 CPD courses will be produced with the following features

- are non-formal open curricula;
- badgable for credentialing;
- recognisable in formal educational settings and by employers;

and a case scenario collection on recognition of validated non-formal open learning.

REMOTE EDUCATION IN MOTHER TONGUE TEACHING AND STUDY GUIDANCE IN MOTHER TONGUE IN JÖNKÖPING COUNTY

Pakitta Kiatkulthorn, Yvonne Lindén Andersson,
Research and Development unit, Region Jönköping County, Sweden

Remote education is currently available in the subjects of mother tongue, modern languages, Sami and sign languages for students in elementary and upper secondary school. According to the Swedish National Agency for Education, remote education is defined as real time and interactive teaching by using information and communication technology (ICT). The students are in schools with a supervisor. The teacher or remote teacher is not in the same location as the students. Remote education is not the same as distance learning, where the students themselves decide when and where they do their schoolwork.

In Sweden, students in elementary and secondary school have the right to receive mother tongue education in case the following conditions are met: (a) one of the student's guardians has a mother tongue other than Swedish, (b) the language is used in everyday communication at home and (c) the student has basic knowledge of that language. Students who are not be able to keep up with education in Swedish language have the right to receive 'study guidance in mother tongue' in one or more subjects. The school principal decides if students need study guidance in mother tongue. However, there are shortages in both mother tongue teachers and study guidance counsellor in several different languages. Thus, not all students who applied for mother tongue teaching were provided with it. Starting from August 1, 2016, school principals are allowed to establish contracts among each other to provide and make use of tuition in mother tongue and study guidance in mother tongue as a service. As a consequence of changed legislation, all 13 municipalities in Jönköping county decided to cooperate in a unique effort to offer students better access to competent teachers in their mother tongue. Thus, it led to the establishment of this remote education project. A coordinator was employed to organize the operation. The coordinator has mapped the demand for languages in the county and trained mother tongue teachers in remote education.

The aim of the project is to coordinate all municipalities in Jönköping county in order to increase the opportunity for students to get their mother tongue teaching or/and study guidance in mother tongue.

The ongoing process shows that the remote education has decreased that gap between demand and supply. The students have better chance to study their mother tongue and to receive study guidance in mother tongue, especially in less common languages. Currently, there are ten languages are now taught remotely by mother tongue teachers in Jönköping county.

GAMIFICATION AS PUBLIC POLICY OF TEACHER TRAINING BY INQUIRY METHODOLOGY

Paula Carolei, UNIFESP, Gislaine Munhoz, SME-SP, Luci Ferraz, ECA-USP, Regina Gavassa, SME-SP, Brazil

This article describes and discusses how gamification was inserted as part of a training policy for teachers who work with technologies in order to boost more investigative performances. It describes and analyses one of the gamified training actions since the gamification elements present in its initial framework and its justifications, the playtest applied in technology managers, and the adjustments made based on the difficulties found in the playtest and also the action performed with eight hundred public school teachers. Bruno Latour's mapping controversies was used as a methodology for analysing the process, highlighting the elements of tension and deepening into the process, identifying the points that need both greater care and attention, and also how the teacher learning can derive from these points of tension.

Our qualitative, mapping methodology registered, described and highlighted the controversies that arose in the design of the gamified activity and its redesign based on the playtest with the managers who acted as mediators in the training. We also brought some more quantitative data from a questionnaire evaluating the experiences that the teachers filled.

We can highlight the following controversies: difficulty in dealing with mistakes; scalability; difficulty with controversial issues; difficulty with more complex and even fantastic narratives; transposition of actions in various technologies; motivation and engagement:

As a mapping process, there is still much to map and our next steps must focus on listening to these teachers and their proposals based on these experiences, as well as a new hearing of mediators and managers after the teachers' production process in training.

But the first conclusions that we can take already give us clear clues that appear in the controversies and show us what points we need to create and innovate to make the gamification something that deepens and helps to realize the process better and its relation with the competences to be developed, and also awaken processes in which the students are more protagonists and take more and more responsibility to make their choices. We propose here a reflection from the training on gamification that goes beyond standardized and reactive logics (or the ones full of distractions) which can cause the student / player to be alienated in such fun, and forget the reason why learning is important.

In addition, our proposal is to promote a greater awareness about the processes and movements of learning, which may be immersive in the experiential impact, but also reflexive in understanding how and why we learn. We want a process in which the student is an agent / actor, but a reflected agency. We propose he makes decisions not by trial and error, but that he is able to explore and analyse the options and choose them consciously. We hope that mistakes and iterativity of the constructions, and also of the act of playing favour the idea of continuous design and improvement. We also hope fun becomes a way to learn from the diverse and that causes you to think differently and not something reductive and alienating that distances you from self-knowledge and the world.

MODERN PROJECT – USEFUL TOOLKIT DEMONSTRATION TO EVALUATE AND USE DIGITAL TOOLS IN EDUCATIONAL SCENARIOS

Alfredo Soeiro, Universidade Porto, Portugal, Carme Royo, Francesca Uras, EUCEN, Spain

Project Goals

The MODERN project aims to help you teach more effectively through incorporating new digital learning tools into your day to day teaching delivery. It is expected MODERN will be a key resource in teacher and trainers' professional development. It has been identified, assessed and categorised the latest and best digital learning tools. This is a project with a website that has actually had real educators looking at and rating every tool. Want to find the best tools for creating courses? Done! Want to find the best tool for testing students? Done! Want to find the best tools for project work? Done! In fact, the unique 10 category classification system makes it easy for anyone to find the best tool for the learning objective that anyone wants to achieve. MODERN has been funded by the European Commission under the ERASMUS+ Programme, so there are no adverts, no sponsors to please, the project is objective and concrete. The project is solely interested in pedagogic potential, not "gimmicks" or commercial gain. By engaging with the project anyone will learn intuitive powerful tools for engaging students, understand the pedagogic potential of digital learning tools, be motivated to incorporate some of these new tools into your teaching practice and increase own digital literacy. MODERN aims to increase the ability and motivation of teachers, trainers and lecturers to use digital learning resources as a means to more effective, relevant teaching, thereby causing a positive impact in students, learners and trainees.

Project Methodology

The project tried to achieve the above goals by providing educators with a convenient and highly usable set of innovative tools which they can use to engage their students on mobile devices, offering clear guidelines on which tool offers the best solutions to achieving pedagogical objectives and presenting project toolkit in a highly attractive manner and user friendly format. Smart phones and tablets have revolutionised the way one lives and works, but not yet in many cases the one teaches students in vocational training or higher education. There are fantastic opportunities however for interactive, student-led learning inside and outside the classroom via these powerful mobile phones. It is known that digital and mobile resources are proven to increase adult learner engagement and information retention. They are also well suited to "hard to reach" learners or those who direct their own learning activities "on the go". Yet only one in five students is taught by digitally confident and supportive teachers. So the project tries to address these issues and newcomers are invited to explore the project site, to take a learning module, to try out a learning tool and to become more digitally confident and capable. The project has developed four resources to help you learn and introduce new digital tools and innovative practice into the teaching and training delivery. Each of the resources is stand alone, but together it is considered they form a holistic package which leads teachers and trainers from the broad objective (Audit of learning tools) to a quite specific output (Online training course). First output is the Audit of Learning Tools. In this report it has been identified, assessed and categorised the latest and best digital learning tools. Since there are endless lists of learning tools out there this project has actually had real educators looking at and rating every tool. Since it is a subjective assessment the option was to have the task led and undertaken by a capable and known university. The second output is the Pedagogic Assessment of the considered as top twenty-five tools. Again the project has categorised the tools in with the ten category classification system. This report presents a more detailed analysis of the pedagogic potential of the tools that were considered most useful. Each assessment is no more than three pages long and provides all the essential information needed to decide if this is a tool that might be useful in a teaching or training activity. Then anyone can learn how to use it, in less than one hour, with the third output called Toolkit! The Toolkit is the third output. It is an online platform designed to teach and train about the top twenty-five. It follows a four-step process: read the pedagogic report, watch the introductory video, view some examples of the impact of the tool in real life learning environments and then learn the tool itself. It is hoped to encourage anyone interested to try one or two of the tools initially, to gauge the impact and then to learn some more tools. The Toolkit is online since December 2016. The fourth output is an Online Training Course to help anyone learn some of these new and innovative teaching digital techniques. It has five modules: Introduction to innovative teaching; The Flipped Classroom teaching model; Collaborative learning spaces and Peer connections; Project based learning; E-learning trends. The relevant aspect of this online training course is that the five modules have been developed using eight of the considered top twenty-five learning tools. Therefore, while taking the modules anyone will gain new knowledge about these tools and also experiment the learning experience of some of these learning tools. It is hoped that the online course will further encourage anyone to implement these tools in their teaching and training delivery.

HOW TO FACILITATE DIVERSITY IN FLEXIBLE LEARNING?

Ulf Sandstrom, Swedish Association for Distance Education (SADE), Sweden, Torhild Slåtto, Flexible Education Norway (FUN), Norway, Airina Volungeviciene, European Distance and E-learning Network (EDEN), United Kingdom and Lithuanian Association of Distance and e-Learning (LieDM association), Lithuania, Ebba Ossiannilsson, Swedish Association for Distance Education, Sweden

Workshop on – How to facilitate diversity in flexible learning

The workshop is dedicated for national associations and their member institutions to discuss how they ensure responsive and responsible facilitation of learners, teachers and institutions on national levels to uptake technology enhanced learning and develop diversity in learning experiences. Technology enhanced learning is today's learning for new groups of students. It changes our learning styles, institutional strategies, teaching and learning skills.

National associations of flexible learning and technology enhanced learning (TEL) professionals are usually the ones who unite professionals applying technologies in learning facilitate learners, teachers and institutions to promote learning using new technologies. Learning should support diversity. The conference theme is "Diversity Matters" we mean this is a very important aspect when developing result oriented learning. It is very important to develop and facilitate application of technologies in learning that support diversity. ICT supported lifelong learning brings individual learning and knowledge, as well as very rationale application of learning results in professional practices.

National associations experience a lot of challenges and requests from local institutions who turn to associations for support to introduce responsible and responsible online learning. Schools and VET organizations, adult and higher education institutions strive for knowledge, practices and quality assurance in online learning applications. There is increasing demand in training institutions and individuals on how responsible and responsibly introduce technology enhanced learning. However, national associations and responsible bodies have rare opportunities to gather and discuss their successes and failures, their instruments and tools, as well as the ways how they facilitate their member institutions and individuals.

Objectives of the workshop

The workshop aims at definition of responsive and responsible facilitation of learners, teachers and institutions on national levels to uptake technology enhanced learning and to develop diversity in flexible learning experiences.

The organized exchange of experiences and practices among national associations should be the kick-off of closer collaboration and networking in the framework of EDEN membership and should evoke synergies of mutual support and sharing. Different experiences and practices presented by national associations should bring together the alliance of professionals to share their problems and solutions in the framework of EDEN membership, and should establish more active networking among associations.

1. Welcome and introduction. Swedish Association for Distance Education (SADE). (5 min)
2. Short presentation of the challenges encountered by Lithuanian Distance and eLearing (LieDM) association. (5 min)
3. Presentation of Flexible Education Norway (FUN), Norway (5 min)
4. Presentation of Foreningen for fleksibel uddannelse FLUID, Denmark (5 min)
5. Presentation of challenges and experiences of e-Learning Development Centre Estonian Information Technology Foundation. Estonia (5 min). After each presentation, the presenters will provide 3 key words – characteristics of the diversity in flexible learning.
6. Introduction to group work (5 min). Ulf Sandstrom, SADE.
7. Group work: mapping the schemes – how do we help flexible learners to experience diversity in learning? How do we create conditions for a diversity in flexible education?

Group work is implemented using online mind mapping and brainstorming at online collaborative document. (15 min)

ENHANCING DIVERSITY WITH OPEN BADGES

Ilona Buchem, Johannes Konert, Beuth University of Applied Sciences Berlin, Germany

Open Badges – competency-aligned digital certificates

This workshop introduces Open Badges as a novel approach and a technical tool to recognise, validate and communicate a diversity of skills and achievements of an individual learner in a digital, verifiable and information-rich format. In an interconnected world we live in, diverse citizens need a way to digitally represent their achievements, experiences, affiliations, skills, competencies and other qualities. So far, traditional certificates and credentials could represent only a minor part of learner's qualities, typically specific knowledge areas. Additionally, they are hard to verify by third parties. School reports, higher education diplomas and certificates of continuing education have been used for a long time now to certify that a learner participated in or completed a course or a program. However, certificates, school grades and workload-based credits tell us nothing about learner's competencies, skills, experiences, motivations or attitudes.

Open Badges are a new concept addressing the weak points of traditional credentialing systems. Open Badges are learner-centred and can be used for micro-credentialing of 21st century skills, including digital skills, creativity, critical thinking, entrepreneurship or team skills, all of which rarely get captured by traditional certificates. Developed as an open standard by Mozilla, Open Badges are connected; verifiable credentials represented in portable image files enriched with metadata and can be combined with digital evidence which demonstrates what it takes to get a badge. In this way, Open Badges represent a more detailed picture than traditional certificates or credits.

Application of Open Badges to reflect diversity of learners

Traditional certificates and credentials have focused on courses, modules and programs but not on the diversity of individual skills, competencies, experiences and achievements. Neither have traditional certificates and credentials reflected the diversity of learners and how to recognize skills of diverse groups of learners and the take into account specific premises of diverse learners which may result from age, gender or cultural background. Traditional certificates and credentials have been also poor in signalling or marking diverse learning pathways which result from a diversity of smaller steps learners take on their learning journey. School grades and workload-based credits tell us nothing about learner's knowledge, skills, experiences, motivations or attitudes. Yet in order to be successful in a networked world of the 21st century, diverse learners need diverse ways of having their skills, achievements and experiences recognized. Moreover, acknowledgement and comparison of achievements, based on traditional credentialing forms, includes manifold manual work, translations and results in barriers for professionals and learners when changing institutions; especially across (European) borders. This is still the case even though the Bologna process has eased the path, but at the same time is limited to higher education only. Open Badges can help to overcome such limitations.

Scenarios

In the underlying workshop the diversity of learners is addressed with Open Badges at three levels: (a) at the level of *diversity of the qualities of a learner* which can be recognized with Open Badges (such as 21st century skills, achievements, affiliations, attitudes, thus going beyond knowledge which is the quality mostly recognized by traditional certificates); (b) at the level of *diversity of learners* themselves, answering the question how Open Badges can help to enhance learning and recognise individual skills of diverse learner groups beyond the pre-defined curriculum. This addresses some of the current challenges such as recognizing skills of migrants and refugees, recognizing skills and promoting learning of girls/women in technology and other STEM fields, or recognizing skills and creating learning opportunities for elderly citizens/workers; (c) at the level of *diversity of learning pathways*, such as creating learning pathways for increasing the depth of expertise, for collaborating across disciplines and learning pathways for career/education changers.

HOW TO CONDUCT AN ACADEMIC CHAT VIA TWITTER

Antonella Poce, Francesco Agrusti, Maria Rosaria Re, Università Roma TRE, Department of Education, Italy

Summary

Exchange of views and research results is a very useful way of growth for everyone. The idea, especially in the academic world, of creating international and interdisciplinary research communities is pivotal and the possibility to access lots of resources, thanks to the wideness and richness of the Web, sometimes makes the identification of useful resources even more difficult and not so easy to manage. Technology can break the boundaries of time and space help and facilitate interaction between people and the Academics. Social media, used every day by people from all over the world, can offer a wide range of possibilities of interaction and exchange of high level information, from FaceBook to Instagram or Twitter.

The workshop *How to conduct an academic chat via Twitter* has the aim to introduce participants in the use of Twitter in scholarly communication, focusing the attention on the #EDENchat case. Individual researchers or Institutions may use twitter for several reasons such as advertising their research, events or publications. No fully comprehensive studies exist on how and why scholars use Twitter and some of them highlight how little use of Twitter is made among scholars. On the other hand, the microblogging on Twitter has become vital to the communication in some fields of research, Web and computer mediated communication for instance. The question is: can a just 140 character academic communication has an impact? Workshop participants will investigate this field and will be instructed in the use of Twitter chat for scholarly and academic communication.

Description of the workshop

The workshop *How to conduct an academic chat via Twitter* has the following objectives:

- to present the characteristic of Twitter chat for scholarly and academic communication;
- to underline the elements (tools, links, references, hashtags) which can promote an academic use of chat via Twitter;
- to invite participants to reflect upon the possibilities to exchange projects and research results via Twitter in order to create an international and interdisciplinary research communities;
- to instruct participants on how to use just 140 characters to communicate and interact with other researcher and students on a specific subject.

The workshop can be also an instrument to engage participants worldwide into the events at EDEN. During the activity, presenters will run simultaneously with a live #EDENchat and all participants can directly learn and use all the information, tools and suggestions to promote the dissemination of part of study and results presented during the 26th EDEN Annual Conference.

RAPID LEARNING DESIGN – THE ABC OF TEACHER ENGAGEMENT AT SCALE

Maria Hedberg, Marita Ljundquist, Lunds universitet, Sweden,
Clive Young, Nataša Perović, University College London, United Kingdom

Overview

How can we best help our time-pressured academics design rich blended and online courses? University College London (UCL) has developed ABC, an effective and engaging hands-on workshop that has now been used with great success across the institution. In just 90 minutes using a rapid prototyping format academic teams work together to create a visual "storyboard" using cards to outline the type and sequence of learning activities, (both online and offline, required to meet the course's learning outcomes. ABC is particularly useful for new courses or those changing to an online or more blended format.

We facilitated *ABC Rapid Blended Course Design for Educators* workshop at EDEN2016 and it raised interest from many institutions, several of them being in Sweden. We will facilitate the workshop at EDEN2017 with our Swedish colleagues who adopted the method and provide an opportunity for interested colleagues from Swedish (and other) universities interested in this method to attend the workshop.

UCL's ABC method

The ABC is a card based method of a curriculum design. The ABC workshop was developed from Viewpoints curriculum design method (Viewpoints project 2008-2012) and takes an activity based approach based on Laurillard's (2012) Learning types. The six learning types are (a) acquisition; (b) inquiry; (c) practice; (d) production; (e) discussion and (f) collaboration, and these form the ABC six-card set. On one side of a card, a learning type is defined (principle) and on the other side are conventional and digital learning activities (practice). At least two members of the team involved in programme or module development attend a workshop. They bring the module specifications (or programme overview) with learning outcomes to the workshop. Several, if not all, modules in a programme are usually addressed in a single session

The conference workshop session would follow the rapid course development format and will introduce participants to ABC tools.

Benefits of ABC

By necessity this rapid-development approach focuses on a simple set of pedagogic principles. Rather than being restrictive this has been found to generate discussion about the fundamental purposes of the programme and foregrounds the student experience. The workshop itself is structured to encourage collective discussion with a focus on collaboration and consensus, starting with the initial 'tweet' exercise. An important aspect of ABC is the staged progression from broad abstraction to concrete activities. Storyboarding provides a visual narrative that teams find easy to work with and the paper-based format encourages creativity and adaptation. The cards themselves act as an aide memoire of potential activities, helping to bring pedagogic diversity to the design. Assessment and feedback also become a natural element of this form of activity-based design rather than driving the module structure. The workshop will show how this method can be used to engage academics.

OPENING UP EDUCATION: FUTURE OF OER AND MOOCS

Ebba Ossianilsson, Swedish Association of Distance Education, Sweden, Cengiz Hakan Aydın, Anadolu University, Fahriye Altınay, Zehra Altınay, Near East University, Turkey

Transformation on education practices

Transformation of education and learning fosters to internalize digital learning environment which there is transition from traditional learning to open up education. Transformation in education and learning itself also put forward to reshape policies and strategies in pedagogy based on change and innovation. Within a framework of life-long learning philosophy, higher education institutions turn attention on new technologies and learner cantered approach for learning and teaching environment to reach global markets based on news form of policies, strategies and quality framework. Opening up education with MOOCs and online learning environments show how transition is proceed as movement on digital learning and how this form of learning provides opportunities for all learners as regarding openness, access and equality. The future and the success of opening up education through OER and MOOCs require quality improvements and movements on both pedagogical and organisational concerns. For the effectiveness of learning and competence development of learners, social interaction, collaboration and empowerment on pedagogical and organisational strategies need to be considered as synergy of online learning and teaching process.

Current practices and future direction on OER and MOOCs

Higher education is facing a range of challenges due to opening up education, the use of OER and MOOCs, and not a least the increased digital transformation, and that the learners have taken the lead of their own learning as learning possibilities are available from everywhere, at any time, and with no costs for anyone. This transformation of learning possibilities worldwide also leads to and requires a leadership leading this transformation by research and practise. The workshop aims to highlight the research debate on following focuses for further researches within the scope of the future of OER and MOOCS: Transformation of education and learning, Digital literacy and learning, Transition from campus education to opening up education, Open online pedagogy principles, Quality indicators of online education, and Open pedagogical and organisational patterns. To improve quality and internationalisation in education, open and distance learning provides life- long learning are essences for equal access and learning opportunities to all learners. It is also strategic innovation and transformation for the higher education institutions to expand the services cross the nations. Therefore, increasing service productivity in open and distance learning requires considering both pedagogical and organisational concerns in synergic manner for the quality improvement. The significant success indicator of the synergy practices relies on organisational support and internalisation of the roles among staff, tutors and the learners. Furthermore, studies point out that instructional principles for all learners need to be considered to provide opportunities of learning for learners with disabilities. This shows how it is significant to use technology in right time and purpose for sustainable development in open and distance learning. Carrying out accreditation and quality studies are crucial to set standards and do performance appraisal for the improvement. Thus, division of responsibilities and professional learning, social interaction, knowledge management framework, service differentiation and strategic policies are the fundamental elements to propose suggestions on future of OER and MOOCs in pedagogical and organisational level.

HOW RELEVANT IS OPEN EDUCATION FOR REFUGEES? EXPERIENCE AND DISCUSSION FROM THE ERASMUS+ PROJECT MOONLITE

Alastair Creelman, Corina Löwe, Linnaeus University, Sweden, Katerina Zourou, Web2Learn, Greece

Objectives of the workshop

The objectives of this workshop are:

- To critically address the relevance of open education for the integration of refugees in Europe
- To discuss and raise awareness of the opportunities that open education offers for the integration and inclusion of refugees
- To harvest good practice and practical applications.

Description

More individuals need to acquire better digital skills and become accustomed to actively using technology to increase their job prospects (EC, Opening up Education, 2013). Participation in open educational offers (such as MOOCs, open educational resources, open courseware) can serve this need. However, there are few examples within the EHEA of institutions strategically deploying MOOCs to complement their own educational offer.

Furthermore, open education can become one support measure in solving the issues the EU is facing with large numbers of incoming refugees. Europe faces a tremendous challenge to support refugees in entering education and employment. Refugees face legal, linguistic, and financial (in countries with high student fees) barriers to enter higher education. Furthermore, traditional universities can only offer places to a certain number of students, with funded places even rarer, and seldom have the capacity to cope with large numbers of refugees in a short time. The lengthy process of seeking asylum is lost time for most refugees. Utilizing MOOCs to support refugees in entering HE or employment market is a strategy to currently being explored by a number of initiatives including Kiron Open Higher Education in Germany. This is in line with ECs communication 2013 "wider use of new technology and open educational resources can contribute to alleviating costs for educational institutions and for students, especially among disadvantaged groups".

The current Erasmus+ project MOONLITE (Massive Open Online courses eNhancing LInguistic and Transversal skills for social inclusion and Employability) aims to address the question of how open education, in particular MOOCs, can offer viable solutions for refugees and contribute to better integration and improved employment prospects. The strategic partnership of MOONLITE specifically aims to:

1. Identify opportunities and barriers for recognizing MOOC-based learning of students and refugees
2. Create institutional and cross-institutional scenarios to exploit MOOCs for credit-bearing HEI courses & future employability among students and refugees
3. Implement a set of scenarios in partner HEIs and among our partnership
4. Study cost and benefits for exploiting informal online courses (focus MOOCs) for 1st and 3rd mission of higher education
5. Run an open online course targeted to MOOC providers and refugees support groups on how to design and utilize MOOCs for refugees while make learning resources available beyond course duration
6. Create a vision and recommendations for a more viable and strategic role of MOOCs in European HEIs.

The workshop contributes to raising critical issues for addressing the integration of refugees in Europe. Despite the number of initiatives taking place in recent years, it seems that the solutions for integration (professional, cultural, linguistic) may not be fully adaptable to the needs of the target population. This workshop helps to enhance a critical thinking into the link between real needs and proposed solutions.

DIGITAL INNOVATION IN CULTURAL AND HERITAGE EDUCATION – THE DICHE WORKSHOP

Antonella Poce, Francesco Agrusti, Maria Rosaria Re, Università Roma TRE, Department of Education, Italy

Summary

The workshop's aim is to promote the use of digital resources in Primary School through cultural and heritage education. Content and structure of the workshop are originated by Erasmus+ KA2 DICHE project (Digital Innovation in Cultural and Heritage Education in the light of 21st century learning). The main objective of the workshop is to instruct participants in the use of the DICHE MENU, an online database of teaching scenarios for cultural and heritage education, which involve the use of digital resources in the development of the 4C skills (Creativity, Communication, Collaboration, Critical Thinking). The aim of integrating digital resources and opportunities in education (especially in the field of cultural and heritage) has to be seen in the light of 21st century learning. In their work titled "21st Century Skills: Learning for Life in Our Times" (2009) Trilling and Fadel create a framework of transversal skills necessary to prepare society for the complex realities of the 21st century. The skills Critical thinking, Creativity, Communication and Collaboration –the 4 C's – are incorporated in the menu. The DICHE scenarios allow children to reflect critically on cultural and heritage issues and to collaborate and communicate in groups in order to come up with creative solutions to the posed problems. In addition to transversal skills, through different assignments that are part of the scenarios, teaching scenarios also pay attention to basic skills such as writing and mathematics. Through the DICHE workshop, teachers, prospective teachers, educators and researchers can also reflect upon the possibilities for digital integration and innovation in their own educational activities.

Description of the workshop

The workshop has the following objectives: to present the DICHE menu of digital tools and set of recommendations in the promotion of digital resources in Primary School through cultural and heritage education; to invite participants to reflect upon the possibilities for digital integration and innovation in their own museum and cultural educational and research activities; to instruct participants on how to use the DICHE menu of digital tools themselves; to guarantee full access to the intellectual outputs of the DICHE project by presenting the online locations on the project partners' websites where they can be accessed.

The DICHE menu is a set of teaching scenarios that promote the use of digital resources and innovative learning method in cultural and heritage education, with the aim to develop transversal skills. By developing and disseminating a menu of teaching scenarios for cultural and heritage education, which involve the use of digital resources, (prospective) teachers, educators and researchers gain access to a set of practical scenarios that they can immediately use in class and in their researcher activities. Integrating the necessary skills to deal with complex 21st century realities in primary school education, such as the 4Cs Critical thinking, Creativity, Communication and Collaboration, asks for innovation. Cultural and heritage education has the potential of integrating 21st century learning in education, whereas digital resources can make cultural and heritage education more appealing to pupils. However, schools and cultural educators struggle to use the full potential of digital learning tools. They invest in digital equipment such as smart boards and tablets, but often use it rather conservatively. Meanwhile, developers of ICT/digital storytelling tools in education aim to make the existing technologies more mainstream in education. Scholars in (digital) innovation in (cultural and heritage) education still face many pending research questions related to the effects of using digital tools and resources in education.

To address the needs of primary schools, teachers, teacher's colleges, parties active in culture and heritage, the ICT/E-learning sector and scholars, this project aims to integrate digital resources and opportunities in primary education in general and in cultural and heritage education in particular. Thus, the workshop supports participants to deliver high quality teaching, to deal with complex classroom realities and to adopt new teaching methods and digital tools.

CREATE YOUR OWN ONLINE LEARNING HUB – A TOOL TO SUPPORT THE DEVELOPMENT OF ONLINE COURSES

Linda Mebus, Nelson Jorge, Willem van Valkenburg, Delft University of Technology, The Netherlands

Improving the quality of TU Delft's open and online education

The Online Learning HUB (https://onlinelearninghub.tudelft.nl) is a platform and community to support the development of open and online education. Created by the Delft University of Technology (TU Delft), its main goal is to improve the quality of open and online education by giving structure to the course development process, making the support more consistent, open and accessible, and embedded in TU Delft's Education Quality Cycle.

Online education is considered critical to the long-term strategy of Higher Education (HE) with consequences for the current professional development policy. While online learning has continued to increase, professional development opportunities for online educators have not been able to keep pace. At the same time most lecturers at brick-and-mortar universities don't have any experience in online teaching and online learning. Improved professional development strategies are needed to facilitate and support faculty to cope with these demands.

Therefore, TU Delft Extension School developed the Online Learning HUB, a platform and community for staff development that supplies operational support for the production of open and online education that complies with quality standards. The purpose is to promote learner-centred professional development which involves teachers (developers, course teams, i.e.) as active and reflective participants.

Is the HUB something for you?

The workshop will present and open up the Online Learning HUB developed to all participants. The workshop aims to explore, test and reflect on an online HUB service for staff development, for higher education institutions that produce (or plan to) and execute online and open education, keeping their staff aligned with the latest developments in the field. The model can be implemented by each individual higher education institution, and connected into a network of institutional models that might speed up the development of open and online education in Europe and worldwide.

Participants will be introduced to the Online Learning HUB and be able to explore its structure and content using their own device, engaging in tasks provided by the presenters. In the second part of the workshop, active participation will be required to conceptualize a new or adapted HUB to their own context/institution, discuss in small groups and in the end present their ideas to all participants and receive feedback.

The workshop will focus on:

- the use the TU Delft Online Learning HUB as a tool to support the development of online courses;
- conceptualizing a HUB for other contexts / institutions;
- compare the way of working of other institutions and discuss the added-value of a HUB.

BOOK OF PROJECTS

Collection of "Synergy" Synopses

e-Schools

Establishing a System for Developing Digitally Mature Schools (pilot project)

e-Škole

Website: https://www.e-skole.hr/en/

Runtime: 03.2015 – 02.2018

Supported / co-funded by: Operational Programme Competitiveness and Cohesion (OPCC), European Regional Development Fund (ERDF), Operational Programme Efficient Human Resources (OPEHR), European Social Fund (ESF)

Partners: CARNet – Croatian Academic and Research Network, HR; University of Zagreb Faculty of organization and informatics, HR; Agency for Vocational Education and Training and Adult Education (ASOO), HR; Croatian Education and Teacher Training Agency (AZOO), HR.

Project representative to be contacted for further info: CARNet office for information and public relations (press@CARNet.hr), Faculty of organization and informatics, Center for international projects.

The e-Schools programme consists of the pilot project, which will be implemented in the 2015-2018 period and the major project, which will be implemented in the 2019-2022 period based on the results of the pilot project. In digitally mature schools, the appropriate use of information and communications technologies (ICT) contributes to the following: an efficient and transparent management of the school (direct objective), the development of digitally competent teachers prepared for the application of innovations in their own pedagogical practices (direct objective), the development of digitally competent students, who are prepared for a continuation of their schooling and competitive on the labour market (indirect objective).

The overall objective of the e-schools programme is to contribute to the capacity building of the primary school and secondary-school educational system in order to allow students to be prepared for the labour market, further education and lifelong learning. The purpose of the e-Schools pilot project is to establish a system for the development of digitally mature schools through the pilot project and the evaluation of the application of ICT (information and communications technologies) in the educational and operational processes of 10% of schools in the Republic of Croatia. The specific objective of the e-Schools pilot project is to pilot organizational, technological and educational concepts of introducing ICT in the educational and operational processes in selected schools during two school years and to develop, based on the experience of the pilot project, a strategy for the implementation of a system of digitally mature schools in the entire primary and secondary education system in the Republic of Croatia, that is for the application in the major project (2019-2022). Experiences on similar European projects for the informatization of operational and teaching processes show that a coordinated implementation is indispensable, regarding both infrastructure and education, with an awareness that the foundation of education is the teacher, and the primary focus the student.

Main target groups of the project: 101 primary schools, 50 secondary schools, more than 23.000 students.

Significant public results: Within the result of the project Digital Maturity of Schools leaded by Assoc. Prof. Nina Begičević Ređep, Ph.D., the Framework for Digital Maturity of Schools (FDMS) and the Instrument for Assessment of Digital Maturity of Primary and Secondary Schools have been developed. The schools can use the FDMS as a guide when planning and integrating the ICT in learning and teaching, as well as in their management processes. The FDMS recognized five areas divided into 38 elements that are described on five digital maturity levels in the form of a rubric. The main five areas of the digital maturity within the FDMS are: (a) Planning, management and leadership, (b) ICT in learning and teaching, (c) Development of digital competences, (d) ICT culture and (e) ICT infrastructure. Each area consists of a larger number of elements which have been described for each maturity level: Basic, Initial, e-Enabled, e-Confident and e-Mature. The FDMS, the Instrument for evaluation of the digitally mature schools and the supporting software represent a unique and comprehensive tool set created according to sound research methodology. Due to their generic characteristics, the FDMS and the Instrument can be applied in other educational systems and countries with minor adjustments. The Instrument can be used as a tool to evaluate the school's digital maturity level but also for the identification of the areas for improvement that could enable the growth on the scale of digital maturity and improve the overall reputation and school results. The FDMS, the Instrument and the accompanying software have been already successfully applied in the process of self-evaluation and external evaluation of 151 schools in Croatia. The significant feedback for improvement of the FDMS and of the Instrument was collected in this validation process. The evaluation of further 1400 elementary and high-schools in Croatia is planned for 2017.

One of the sub-results of the project result “Improved, transparent and connected business and teaching processes of schools” is “Learning Analytics and Educational Data Mining”, leaded by Full Prof. Blaženka Divjak, Ph.D. The main aim of this project sub-result is the development of National Learning Analytics (LA) and Data Mining System for pre-tertiary education system in Croatia. In order to ensure that main groups of users of Learning Analytics System get what they need the most by using learning analytics, within this project sub-result is developed the methodology for needs analysis for Learning Analytics System for pre-tertiary education system and it was implemented in primary and secondary schools in Croatia during 2016. The approach consists of the following phases: (a) setting of overall objectives and vision of the LA System with the primarily focus on improving students learning and motivation but also to support schools in accountability and national authorities in setting, monitoring and evaluating the strategic goals, (b) user needs analysis (identified six main groups of users: Students/pupils and their parents; Teachers; School management and support (principal / pedagogue / psychologist); Local and national education authority (School founders / Ministry / Agencies for Quality Assurance); Policy making bodies and researchers and Project partners on “E-schools” project), (c) data availability analysis, (d) dashboards development (setting aims for dashboard for each identified user group and designing dashboard functionalities with user evaluation of examples of dashboard design and functionalities) and (e) tender specification.

The central part of Learning Analytics System is Data Analysis System. Very important part of the LAS is also the Consent System that allows students and teachers finer control of how their personal data is used. Further, the System for Warning and Intervention helps students and teachers to deal with risks, and finally Success Planner enables the development of students’ planning competencies and other metacognitive skills.

DCU-Fuse

DCU-Fuse: 24-Hour Online Envisioning Activity

DCU

NIDL National Institute for Digital Learning

Website: https://www.dcufuse.ie

Runtime: 30.03.2017 – 31.03.2017

Supported / co-funded by: Dublin City University

Partners: ADAPT Centre, DCU Office for Quality Promotion, National Institute for Digital Learning, Ireland

Project representative to be contacted for further info: Professor Mark Brown (mark.brown@dcu.ie)

Short description: At the end of March, Dublin City University (DCU – www4.dcu.ie) embarked on an innovative digital learning initiative, which saw the university's staff, students, alumni, key stakeholders and friends of the DCU family take part in an online discussion to help shape the next phase of the University's development. DCU Fuse (https://www.dcu.ie/news/2017/mar/s0317s.shtml) was a 24-hour online envisioning and consultation process, including a number of special distinguished guests from around the world, such as Professor George Siemens (http://linkresearchlab.org/about/staff/), to gather ideas on some of the opportunities and challenges facing higher education in the future. The objective was to use new technology to canvas the DCU community for ideas and suggestions to contribute to the University's new Strategic Plan (2017-2022). The conversation coincided with Open Education Week (www.openeducationweek.org) and was open to university's 17,000 students, 1,200 staff and 80,000 graduates and members of the wider public. A team of moderators were assigned to each conversation over the 24-hour period. Their role was to monitor the conversation and ensure that the experience was undertaken in a constructive, enjoyable, friendly and non-threatening environment. The following video explains more about DCU-Fuse: https://www.youtube.com/watch?v=qVw03wcjc4k

Figure 1. Example of a DCU-Fuse conversation

Main target groups of the project: Staff, students, alumni, key stakeholders and members of the public.

Significant public results: Over the 24-hour period there were around 70,000 page views, over 5,000 discussion posts, more than 7,000 likes, and DCU-Fuse trended as high as number 2 in Ireland on Twitter.

Figure 2. Final post by the University President

Figure 3. An initiative widely embraced by DCU staff

WikiWelcome

Students learn and share knowledge about their local communities in open online environments

Website: https://sv.wikiversity.org/wiki/V%C3%A4lkommen_till_min_plats

Runtime: 01.2016– 12.2016

Supported / co-funded by: Main grant is from Vinnova (Swedish agency for innovation) "Innovation projects for the future of education", co-funded by Wikimedia Sverige and City of Stockholm

Partners: Wikimedia Sverige, Stockholmskällan (Digital archive for schools part of City of Stockholm), and Swedish National Heritage Board, Sweden.

Project representative to be contacted for further info: Sara Mörtsell (sara.mortsell@wikimedia.se)

This project is an example of how open platforms and cultural institutions can support K-12 education to develop pedagogies and collaborations to foster diversity in online participation of public spaces. 230 students in K-12 education from both minority and dominant communities in the city of Stockholm participated in 2016. The topic is the school's local geography, culture and historic environment, encouraging a pedagogical approach of examining the local neighbourhood's past, present and future. Digital platforms and media in the project are commons driven and under CC by or CC by-sa licenses. Three main platforms are involved – the national website platsr.se, run by the Swedish National Heritage Board, the free encyclopedia for children wikimini.se and the Swedish language version of the free encyclopedia Wikipedia. The Wikipedia education program, actively running in Sweden since 2013, positions students as collaborators and knowledge producers in the world's largest encyclopedia while developing digital literacies characterised by a resident mode of online engagement. This OER project takes its starting point in the Wikipedia program and adds a pedagogical framework to support complexity in terms of diversity of linguistic genres and difference of perspectives, such as dealing with facts and opinions. Incentives from teachers who joined the project from outer city schools were founded on the willingness to teach students that their knowledge and expertise of their local area and communities count, and how to take action to validate it and claim ownership of the historic environment and the diversity of traces it holds. Such ideas connect classroom activities in open online environments with aspects of critical pedagogy.

One of the key insights from the project is that stakeholders groups of education, such as public bodies (cultural heritage institutions, archives, museums) and NGOs such as Wikimedia, have the opportunity to bring open knowledge and platforms to educational settings to support underrepresented groups and voices real-world impact in sustainable digital projects and develop literacies for a digital age.

Main target groups of the project: K-12 educators in outer city schools of Stockholm, education programs at cultural institutions, open education advocates

Significant public results:

- The project's portal page at Swedish Wikiversity contains results and instructions as an OER (Open educational resource) https://sv.wikiversity.org/wiki/V%C3%A4lkommen_till_min_plats.
- Videos with teacher interviews and classroom activities to be published in February 2016.

CRITHINKEDU

Critical Thinking across the European Higher Education Curricula

Website: http://crithinkedu.utad.pt

Runtime: 09.2016 – 08.2019

Supported / co-funded by: Erasmus+ / Cooperation for innovation and the exchange of good practices

Partners: CRITHINKEDU Coordinator: Universidade de Trás-Os-Montes e Alto Douro (Portugal), see more at: http://crithinkedu.utad.pt/en/our-team/

Project representative to be contacted for further info: Caroline Dominguez (carold@utad.pt)

Critical Thinking (CT) education is today of utmost importance for universities in the preparation of future workers and participatory citizens. Employers frequently complain about the existing gaps between the competency profiles of graduates and labour market needs, in particular with respect to those called "soft skills". Current changes in society, mainly due to the rapid technological innovation, make hard skills obsolete in searching for new solutions to complex problems and tasks. Efforts need to focus on the development and daily practice of soft skills, less tangible to quantify, which include the ability for complex thinking (e.g. taking initiatives and solving problems); interpersonal communication and participatory learning (e.g. team-working, communication and leadership); personal shaping of knowledge (e.g. progressive mastery, internal drive/motivation, long-life learning); and managerial abilities – that will make individuals ready for today's dynamic and unpredictable career paths.

Growing European awareness of this concern led to the inclusion of generalistic critical thinking subjects in university curricula, along with an attempt to change the pedagogical methods and a closer collaboration with experts and companies for curriculum reform and redefinition of learning outcomes. Nevertheless, even though promoted by educational policies, the opportunities to develop CT skills (which are not intuitive) are generally scarce and undervalued within European Higher Education Institutions {EHEI) standardized curricula – which still, in a large part, underline the memorization, retrieval and transmission of knowledge. Also, the offer of specific semestral courses on CT generalities may not bridge the existing gap [8]. As stated by [9], the gains of a large proportion of students in critical thinking, complex reasoning and written communication are either exceedingly small or empirically non-existent.

Research on intervention studies reinforces the need for good (empirically investigated) instructional approaches in CT, increasing teacher training and professional development on this matter, with focus on course design and implementation – ensuring the favourable conditions and requirements to enhance CT in their students. This is not only because CT has a disciplinary component which makes the concept difficult to define, but also because lecturers don't know how to teach it or how effective their approach is (see "Pedagogy of hope").

In this sense, CRITHINKENDU arises from the background and experience of 11 EHEI and NGO's on the continuous concern to improve the quality of learning in universities, across different sectors, which converge in a common need on how to better support the development of CT education according to the labour market needs and challenges. More specifically, it intends to:

- Connect EHEI, NGOs and companies to identify their common expectations and needs, aligning an collection of CT learning outcomes with the current labour market challenges in different European countries;
- Define standardized guidelines and instructional approaches to teach and assess CT across the different EHEI courses, properly aligned with the inventory of learning outcomes;
- Deliver a model/framework of specific CT training and learning activities to faculty teachers and students, across different domains and disciplines, based on the previous defined guidelines and instructional approaches, increasing faculty professional development and support teaching modernization in EHEI;
- Propose quality assurance criteria for CT education, through a set of recommendations to promote and embed it across universities, supporting policy reforms in the EHEI curricula;
- Create a European network with EHEI, NGO's and companies, to disseminate and share best practices, recommendations, quality criteria and research papers on CT education.

CRITHINKEDU will create the opportunity to foster dialogue among relevant actors from society {sometimes forgotten), in a joint 'industry-university' forum, with a continuous effort to align learning outcomes with real world challenges. It will also allow the implementation of a model of CT teaching and learning activities transnationally, in the different partners' courses, and the consortium will work as a sort of Foundation to promote CT education around Europe. This internationalization of CT curricula should be an effective way of providing an academic environment that supports the diverse cultural learning needs of international students – preparing them to be successful in today's interdependent global society.

Main target groups of the project: Higher education

t-MAIL

Teacher Mobile Application for Innovative Learning

Website: http://www.tmailproject.eu/

Runtime: November 2015 – October 2017

Supported / co-funded by: Erasmus+ KA3, Support for policy reform; Prospective initiatives; Forward looking cooperation projects

Partners: Vrije Universiteit Brussel (Coordinator), BE; Universidad Autonoma de Madrid, ES; University of Hull, UK; Universitaet Wien, AT; Youth Entrepreneurial Service Foundation, Former Yugoslav Republic of Macedonia (MK); Het Gemeenschapsonderwijs, BE; European Distance and E-Learning Network, UK; Kidimedia bvba, BE; ETUCE-CSEE, BE.

Project representative to be contacted for further info: Dr. Jeltsen Peeters (jeltsen.peeters@gmail.com) – project coordinator

t-MAIL aims to develop and test a mobile application supporting primary school teachers, teacher educators and educational decision makers in implementing classroom practices that stimulate students' self-regulated learning (SRL). The project aims to address the needs of these different target groups by designing activities to support the development and testing of a mobile app. It delivers a personalized training course on SRL for in-service primary school teachers. Data generated through the mobile app will be processed through learning analytics and semantics. This approach, in support of data-driven teacher education, will enable the personalization of teachers' and students' learning, ultimately facilitating evidence-based policy making pathways. The mobile training app and associated feedback loops will be piloted and evaluated in three European countries, the UK, Belgium and Spain. Materials will be available in English, German, French, Spanish, Dutch, and Macedonian.

Main target groups of the project:

- Primary school teachers;
- Teacher educators, trainers;
- Educational decision makers.

Significant public results:

- Project results;
- Theoretical framework report;
- Stakeholder study report;
- Repository course material;
- Country reports on educational policy;
- Mobile application;
- Teacher training course;
- Pilot study;
- Evaluation report.

LIST

Learning Content for Smartphones and Tablets

Website: http://www.doflillebaelt.dk, https://myoutime.com/myoutimes, http://www.sverd.se

Runtime: 08. 2016 – 10.201

Supported / co-funded by: Nordplus Voksen2016, the Nordic Council of Ministers

Partners: DOF, Lillebaelt, DK; The Swedish Association for Distance Education, SE; Conexus AS, NO.

Project representative to be contacted for further info: Ebba Ossiannilsson (Ebba.Ossiannilsson@gmail.com)

The digital transformation is progressing rapidly in society. Most people use mobile devises today, particularly to create and maintain a presence online. Hence, the delivery of learning content via these mobile devises is a topical issue in terms of both pure distance learning and situations where online-based teaching materials supplement traditional teaching. New solutions are being developed continuously to exploit this potential.

The purpose of this project is to provide teachers and managers of adult learning with knowledge about these solutions and the practical skills needed to apply them. Content disseminated on mobile devises must be more dynamic and updated more frequently than content that is distributed via websites. Online learning materials cannot be simply transferred to mobile devices. It is important for teachers to apply the tools needed to develop self-generating learning materials in order to achieve self-determined learning for students. Thus, the project's preliminary goal is to map relevant technologies and solutions that meet the needs and challenges of adult pedagogy (i.e., andragogy and heutagogy). Based on the results, courses are then designed for these target groups. Within the framework of the project, at least one test run of the courses is carried out. Both the results of the survey distributed to the users (i.e., learners and teachers) and the tested courses then will be used in the daily work of the partner institutions in all three Scandinavian countries, which will be possible because the Scandinavian language is used and understood in these countries. The courses will be built in the Norwegian mYouTime by the Norwegian partner, Conexus. The project extends projects that were previously conducted by DOF Lillebealt in Denmark with support from NORDPLUS Adult and financial support from the Nordic Council of Ministers, which has developed mobile courses in collaboration with Nordic partners.

Main target groups of the project: Adult learners, adult educators, general and vocational learners, formal, informal and/or non-formal adult learners

Significant public results: (events, reports, tools, repositories, case studies, recommendations, etc.)

The project will yield two tangible products: (a) a report that summarizes the existing knowledge of the tools and technologies available for mobile learning; (b) a training course that targets groups that practice or will work in mobile learning.

Overall, these two products will increase the awareness of the providers of adult education of the demand for the delivery of learning content on mobile devices. The products also will lead to the creation of a group of actors with practical skills in the field. The main goal of the project is that it will contribute significantly to creating a critical mass of practitioners that are active in mobile learning, which will form the basis for shifting e-learning from PC-based platforms to mobile devices as the users move their online presence from their personal computers to their mobile devices. The focus of the project will be on disseminating tools that do not require specialist knowledge in the field of mobile learning and that can be used by a wide range of teachers in applying their professional skills. The evaluation of this project will be based on the qualitative and quantitative feedback from users, which will be used to optimize the courses for daily use.

HigherDecision

Development of a methodological framework for strategic decision-making in higher education – a case of open and distance learning implementation

Website: http://higherdecision.foi.hr

Duration: 06.2015 – 05.2019

Supported / co-funded by: Croatian Science Foundation

Partners: University of Zagreb, Faculty of Organization and Informatics (project coordinator), HR; University of Split, University Computing Center – SRCE, HR; K.U. Leuven, BE; University of Edinburgh, UK, etc., see: http://higherdecision.foi.hr/en

Project representative to be contacted for further info: Blaženka Divjak (bdivjak@foi.hr)

Higher education's (HE) key mission is to develop human potential with beneficial effects for social and economic development. HE as a system, along with HE institutions, must be innovative and strategically managed to be able to fulfil their mission. Therefore, the decision making accompanied by evaluation of its implementation in higher education is an issue of highest priority. Two basic components of this project are defined as follows:

1. Development of methodological framework for strategic decision making and monitoring of its implementation;
2. Application, adjustment and evaluation of our methodology on the example of decision implementation on e-learning and distance learning.

The research on decision making is structured as a cycle of strategic decision making with four phases:

1. Intelligence – problem identification and research, advancement of methodologies such as readiness assessment, diffusion of innovation, etc.
2. Design of methodology – design of decision making methodology and decision making, improvement of multicriteria decision analysis enabling better strategic decision making in HE.
3. Implementation and monitoring – research and identification of key factors that determine effectiveness of strategic decision, their correlation, design of measuring model for maturity and effectiveness of strategic decision implementation in HE.
4. Evaluation – survey possible approaches and evaluation by application of J. Pearl's structural causal models for identification of effects of strategic decision as well as learning analytics.

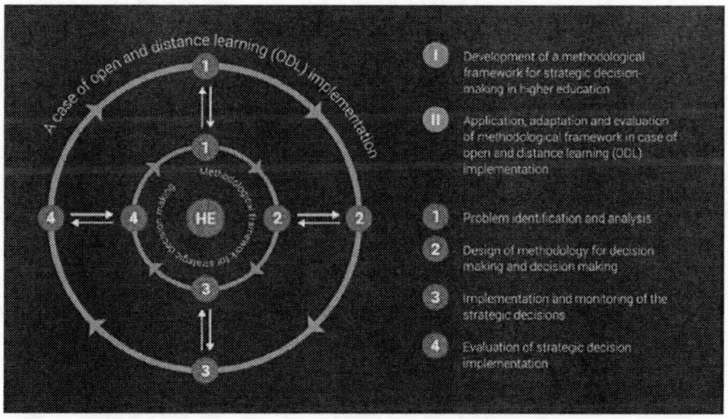

Main target groups of the project: higher education leaders, national and international policy and decision makers in HE, curriculum developers, ODL researchers and teachers in HE

Significant public results: available at http://higherdecision.foi.hr/en/results

OBServatory

International Observatory on Online Higher Education in Management

Website: http://www.obs-edu.com/es/noticias/noticia/obs-presenta-el-2o-informe-del-international-observatory-online-higher-education-management, http://observatory.obs-edu.com

Runtime: 02.2017 – 12.2020

Supported / co-funded by: OBS Business School

Partners: Universidad Virtual y Nacional de Quilmes, AR; Fundaçao Getulio Vargas Online, BR; CEDaD Universidad presbiteriana Mackenzie, BR; Universidad de Shanghai, CN; Universidad EAN, CO; Politecnico Grancolombiano, CO; Pontificia Universidad Javeriana – Bogotá, CO; Universidad EAFIT Virtual, CO; Universidad Autónoma del Caribe, CO; Universidad Santo Tomás, CO; Fundación Universitaria CEIPA, CO; Aosta Valley University, IT; Tecnológico de Monterrey, MX; Universidad Virtual de Guadalajara, MX; Universidad Anáhuac México Sur, MX; Universidad UMAD, campus Virtual, MX; Nnamdi Azikiwe University, NG; Universidad Peruana de Ciencias Aplicadas – UPC, PE; University of Évora, PT; Srinakharinwirot University, TH.

Project representative to be contacted for further info: Eulalia Torras (eulalia.torras@onlinebschool.com)

HOME: OBServatory is an initiative of the OBS Business School. This community aims to share professional experience in online higher education in order to create a space for dialogue and exchange and collaborative research that allows for a broad view of online higher education in management, the main tendencies of the future and the challenges to be faced. In view of this, the OBServatory fulfils its annual commitment to publish and share some of the most relevant information resulting from the research and the debate promoted through the network. The report is provided as a communication tool to foster dialogue between institutions, professionals, providers and students among many other key players who are affected by the decisions of online higher educational institutions.

REPORTS: OBServatory publishes annual reports with results on online learning processes obtained with members' collaboration. These reports are accessible in this section.

NEWS: Periodically news about participation in conferences, collaborations and outstanding publications are include.

MEMBERS: The list of collaborators is included in the previous section.

WIKI: Online space to submit questionnaires and discuss trends in higher education in management.

PAPERS & PRESENTATIONS: The members academic production has its visualization in this space.

COLLABORATIONS: OBServatory collaborates with academic publications such as editors and reviewers.

Main target groups of the project: an international community of deans, managers, teachers and researchers in online higher education in the area of management and business management.

Significant public results: Attendance at conferences, academic papers, publications, seminars and annual reports.

Please note that, at present, you can find the information about International Observatory on Online Higher Education in Management in the link mentioned above. Direct access via observatory.obs-edu.com is currently under construction and it is expected to be fully operative by the end of March 2017.

WISR16

Web-based courses for international positioning of strategic research groups

Website: http://www.kau.se

Runtime: 01.2017 – 12.2019

Supported / co-funded by: Knowledge Foundation, Sweden; NU 16 – Online Education for International Positioning

Partners: BillerudKorsnäs AB, SE; Inission AB, SE; Macforum AB, SE; Pollen AB, SE; Idea2Innovation Sweden AB, SE; Rolls-Royce AB, SE; Sentor MSS AB, SE; Valmet AB, SE.

Project representative to be contacted for further info: Jörg Pareigis (jorg.pareigis@kau.se)

Karlstad University has a vision to be internationally acknowledged for excellence in several research fields and to be at the forefront of some of them. Towards this end, a strategic realignment of the research prioritization strategy has been taken place with a long-term financial commitment to strategically important research groups. After a comprehensive evaluation that took place during the fall of 2013 and 2015, two excellent research groups and five strong research groups were nominated. The University's educational strategy focuses on high quality teaching, flexible forms of study and professional contacts. To further strengthen the ties between research and education and in support of our blended learning strategy, Karlstad University answered a call by the Knowledge Foundation, Sweden, as part of the online education for international positioning programme. The aim of the project is to profile and position these strategic groups through web-based courses. The project builds on the recently adopted strategy for online courses for the strategic research groups of the University, which can be regarded as an integration of our educational and research strategy.

The deliverables of the project are four modularized courses on advanced level with a combined scope of 27 ECTS, aimed at different target groups in the Swedish and international business arena. Building on earlier achievements from the Knowledge Foundation financed project use.it, the courses will be developed as hybrid open online courses. A hybrid open online course design combines the advantages of providing targeted courses on advanced level, with the advantages of massive open online courses and enables the University to list the courses in international course databases such as Class Central and thereby raising our international visibility and profile. Towards this end, we will also produce and disseminate a variety of open educational resources (OERs), many in the form of short video lectures. For each course, we recruited one to three companies who will actively contribute to the course development and ensure the highest possible match to business sector needs, while the hybrid format supports scalable lifelong learning.

To support the course development and production, the project will recruit external experts. This will lead to an accelerated competence development of our researchers in terms of online teaching techniques, which is another central focus area of the project. Experiences from the start of the cross-faculty course development project as well as its predecessor will be shared in this project presentation.

Main target groups of the project: Business professionals, Educational technologists, Faculty

Significant public results: Several dozens of high quality open educational resources have been developed so far, as part of three hybrid open online courses on advanced level in the area of service management and marketing, which are also published with a CC-BY license.

eLene4work

Learning to learn for new digital soft skills for employability

Website: http://www.eLene4work.eu

Runtime: December 2014 – October 2017

Supported / co-funded by: Erasmus+ KA2: Cooperation for innovation and the exchange of good practices, Strategic Partnerships addressing more than one field

Partners: Coordinator: Fondazione Politecnico Di Milano, IT; see the full list of partners: http://elene4work.eu/project-description-2/list-of-partners/

Project representative to be contacted for further info: Project coordinator: Matteo Uggeri (matteo.uggeri@polimi.it)

The aim of the eLene4work project is to help students and new entrepreneurs develop soft skills (often also referred to as 21st century skill, such as problem solving, learning to learn, cooperation, effective and clear communication, adapting to different cultural contexts, managing conflicts, showing endurance in complicated or stressful situations, etc.). The eLene4work outputs and services, therefore, are aimed to help companies exploit the digital talents of young employees. The project proposes a strategic partnership whose goal is to test and monitor the possibility offered by various means of open and distance learning opportunities such as MOOCs and OER to address the demand for digital soft skills (like e-collaboration, digital communication, social network participation, social media management and web 2.0 activities in general) formally not taught at universities but desirable by most employers on the labour market.

The aim of the eLene4work project is to allow students to:

- autonomously identify their own:
  - gaps in soft skills and competences, in order to develop or improve them;
  - potential in digital soft skills, to increase their professional attractiveness on the labour market;
- autonomously learn how to:
  - fill their skill gap using MOOCs (and other OERs)
  - include in their CV their soft skills and digital soft skills in order to enhance the opportunity to enter the labour market.

Main target groups of the project:

- VET institutions and universities (deans, presidents, rectors, teachers as well as students);
- managers, HRs, entrepreneurs, chambers of commerce and company;
- instructional designers, e-learning experts, researchers and policy makers.

Significant public results: The main results of eLene4work are the following:

- Comparative analysis on state of the art on soft skills and soft skills 2.0:
- Focus groups with the stakeholders;
- Self-evaluation tool;
- Orientation guide for students and young workers;
- Personal Journal;
- Lesson learned kit.

OBN

Open Badge Network

Website: http://www.openbadgenetwork.com

Runtime: September 2014 – August 2017

Supported / co-funded by: Erasmus+, KA2, Strategic Partnerships in the field of Higher Education

Partners: Beuth-Hochschule fuer Technik Berlin, DE; Cambridge Professional Development, UK; EDEN – European Distance and E-Learning Network, UK; Dienst Uitvoering Onderwijs, NL; Institute for Sustainable Technologies – National Research Institute, PL; Digitalme, UK, ARTES – Applied Research into Training and Education Systems, IT. Associated partner: University of Applied Sciences and Arts of Southern Switzerland, SUPSI, CH.

Project representative to be contacted for further info: Prof. Dr. Ilona Buchem (buchem@beuth-hochschule.de)

The Open Badge Network (OBN) is an Erasmus+ project which brings together organisations from across Europe to support the development of an Open Badge ecosystem, promoting the use of Open Badges to recognise non-formal and informal learning.

Mozilla Open Badges is an open standard that allows all skills and achievements to be recognised and shared across the web. Schools, Universities, Employers and informal learning providers globally are using open badges to capture lifelong learning which is currently unrecognised.

This project aims to provide a trusted source of independent information, tools and informed practice to support people who are interested in creating, issuing and earning badges across Europe.

We are looking for organisations and individuals from across Europe to join us and help build the Open Badge Network. It doesn't matter whether you are a badge novice or expert, you can become a member of the Open Badge Network by registering here: OBN community registration (http://www.openbadgenetwork.com/members/register/).

Main target groups of the project:

- Educational and human resource professionals;
- Employers and self-employed professionals and organisations;
- Organisations and learning communities where educational practitioners and leaders operate (educational institutions, businesses, public and private, small and large);
- Local, regional and national authorities, policy makers;
- Citizens at different stages of their education and life in a perspective of lifelong and life-wide learning;
- Professionals working with disadvantaged groups (learners with special needs, school push/drop out, women back to work, unemployed, migrants, etc.);
- Sister initiatives / projects (e.g. ODS, LeHo, VM-PASS, OpenPROF, ReOpen, EBA, etc.);
- Institutions, organisations who have influence and/or commitment in the recognition of informal learning and in-demand workplace skills.

Significant public results:

- Creation of an Open Badges European professional network;
- Open Badges MOOC (Massive Open Online Course);
- Open Badges initiatives to support learning regions and cities;
- Open Badges infrastructure;
- Integration of Open Badges at policy level, in particular with the Europass initiative.

ReOpen

Recognition of Valid and Open Learning

Website: http://reopen.eu

Runtime: **01-11-2016** to **31-10-2018**

Co-funded by: Erasmus + KA2 Cooperation for Innovation and the Exchange of Good Practices – Strategic partnerships for vocational education and training

Partners: Vytautas Magnus University (Project coordinator), LT; ONECO, ES; ESCP Europe Wirtschafthochschule, DE; Q21 – Agentur für Qualifizierungs und Transfermanagement GmbH, DE; SRCE – Sveuciliste u Zagrebu Sveucilisni Racunski Centar, HR; EDEN – European Distance and e-Learning Network, UK.

Project representative to be contacted for further info: Airina Volungevičienė (airina.volungeviciene@vdu.lt)

Short Description

The ReOpen project addresses the following priorities:

- Open and innovative education, training and youth work, embedded in the digital era;
- Transparency and recognition of skills and qualifications to facilitate learning, employability and labour mobility;
- Access to training and qualifications for all through C-VET.

Opening Up education – apart from the need for structural changes – also created challenges and opportunities in curriculum opening up represented by

- Open Educational Resources;
- Massive Open Online Courses;
- open collaboration and communication among teachers and learners;
- creating innovative education services for diverse learning groups;
- recognition and validation of non-formal open learning.

The ReOpen project follows recommendations stated in the EC JRC research study on "Validation of Non-formal MOOC-based learning" (2016) by establishing validated open learning practices.

According to this study, to recognize non-formal open learning, education institutions and employers need

- validated Open Online Learning (OOL) curriculum examples;
- digitally smart learning environments leading to OOL recognition and
- case scenarios on recognition of validated non-formal open learning.

Scope of the project:

- addressing objectives of "Opening Up";
- implementing recommendations of EC JRC research study by
  - establishing validated open learning practices;
  - offering learner credentials for online and open learning (OOL) by
  - verification of learner identity;
  - setting learning agreement and other instruments;
  - establishing digital badges for recognition of learning achievements;
  - establishing collaboration with institutions to provide transparent information on potential recognition of OOL;
  - providing teacher training with the tools for OOL development and recognition.

Significant public results:

- an online platform for non-formal open learning curriculum development with learning validation and recognition instruments in place (learner credentials, digital badges, learning path recognition and assessment tools);
- training materials for teachers and trainers in (C-)VET, HE, companies and adult learning organisations on
  - designing non-formal open learning curriculum;
  - application of digital badges for credentialing the learning achievements;
  - recognition of non-formal open learning in formal curricula;
- short term joint staff training event;
- collaboration with institutions to provide transparent information on potential recognition of OOL;
- 5 CPD courses with the following features
  - are non-formal open curricula;
  - badgable for credentialing;
  - recognisable in formal educational settings and by employers;
- a case scenario collection on recognition of validated non-formal open learning.

BizMOOC

Knowledge Alliance to enable a European-wide exploitation
of the potential of MOOCs for the world of business Programme

Website: http://bizmooc.eu

Runtime: 01.2016-12.2018

Supported / co-funded by: Erasmus+ | Key Action 2 | Knowledge Alliances | Reference Number: 562286-EPP-1-2015-1-AT-EPPKA2-KA

Partners: BizMOOC is coordinated by JOANNEUM Graz, University of Applied Sciences, Graz, AT; The consortium (http://bizmooc.eu/consortium/) consists of 11 full partners and 3 associate partners out of 11 countries deriving from HEIs & Industry (large companies & SMEs), NGOs, networks, cluster.

Project representative to be contacted for further info: Christian Friedl – FH JOANNEUM (christian.friedl@fh-joanneum.at) and Darco Jansen – EADTU (darco.jansen@eadtu.eu)

BizMOOC tackles the European challenge of enabling businesses, labour force and universities to increase their activities and exploitation (economies of scale) of the MOOC potential. It focuses on work force & HEI-training and the acquisition of labour market key competences through applying new methodologies for online teaching & learning. This will be achieved by creating common standards & frameworks on MOOCs by integrating the experiences from Higher Education and the business world.

Main target groups of the project: BizMOOC benefits businesses, HEIs, teachers, learners & policy-makers through the core results MOOC BOOK (business & quality models, methods & tools, IPR strategies, certification, competence-based education etc.), Pilot MOOCs, BizMOOC Community & events.

Significant public results: Whatever you need to know about Massive Open Online Courses (MOOCs) is now available in a MOOC BOOK (http://mooc-book.eu), the free online resource to MOOCs for businesses, workforce and universities.

The first edition of this MOOC BOOK already has over 400 pages and includes guidelines, state-of-the art papers, good practices and recommendations how to apply MOOCs. In addition, results of a survey with over 1.000 respondents and the analysis of the more than 100 interviews conducted are published as part of the MOOC BOOK.

MOOC BOOK 1.0 is online available but a pdf of the whole book or subsections can be downloaded with an open license. You will learn about opportunities for the use of MOOCs, comment and discuss hot topics such as quality, business models or certification with a growing business community.

The outcomes (http://bizmooc.eu/outcomes/) are BizMOOC project until April 2017 are

- Report "State of the Art on existing MOOC knowledge", consisting of 14 discussion papers;
- Three reports on needs and gaps for the three target groups of BizMOOC;
- Three Guidelines for Business, HEIs and Labour Force/Society/Learners.

All these results are integrated in the MOOC BOOK (http://mooc-book.eu).

Based on this, 3 Pilot MOOCs focusing on LLL (life-long learning) and business key competences "Learning to learn (through MOOCs)", "sense of initiative (entrepreneurship & intrapreneurship)" and "innovation, creativity & problem-solving" will be developed to test different methods & didactical approaches.

ARMAZEG

Developing Tools for Lifelong Learning in the Transcaucasus Region: e-Learning

ARMAZEG
Developing tools for lifelong learning inTranscaucasus region: e-Learning

Website: http://www.armazeg.com/en

Runtime: December 2013 – May 2017

Supported / co-funded by: Tempus

Partners: Katholieke Universiteit Leuven, BE (coordinator); State Engineering University of Armenia, AM; Ministry of Education and Science of the Republic of Armenia, AM; Institute of Informatics & Automation Problems of NAS RA, AM; Orbeli Institute of Physiology of NAS RA, AM; Armenian State Pedagogical University after Kh. Abovian, AM; St. Andrew the First-Called Georgian University, GE; Georgian Technical University, GE; Università degli Studi di Firenze, IT; University of Granada, ES; European Distance and E-Learning Network, UK; Ivane Javakhishvili Tbilisi State University, GE.

Project representative to be contacted for further info: Ilse Op de Beeck (ilse.opdebeeck@kuleuven.be)

Financed by the European Commission within the TEMPUS program the ARMAZEG project aims to stimulate educational reform in Armenian and Georgian partner universities by establishing e-Learning centres and training for their staff members – with special attention to lifelong learning methodologies.

The project involves twelve partners from Europe and Transcaucasia with a clear vision to establish new links in the educational sphere between the two regions. With the assistance of four European partners ARMAZEG's Armenian and Georgian institutions will import and adapt e-Learning practices in their educational agenda to realise a flexible organisation of higher and adult education locally. A thorough needs analysis accompanied by study visits to the state of the art European universities will help the Transcaucasian partners improve learning by supporting student-centred methodologies, support research-based higher education and enable the internationalisation of their higher education services.

Amongst the most important outcomes of the project will be the establishment of e-learning centres in 7 partner universities of Armenia and Georgia and the implementation of pilot projects in different disciplines. To ensure the sustainability of the concept in Transcaucasian partner institutions, the project also includes, besides the above mentioned policy makers' study visits, trainings of trainers and regional and national workshops.

Main target groups of the project: Higher education stakeholders (University management, lecturers, administration staff, students)

Significant public results:

- Documents:
  - State-of-the-Art report on Armenian and Georgian e-learning (available);
  - Policy recommendations regarding e-learning and ICT for LLL in Armenia and Georgia;
  - Long-term capacity building strategy regarding e-learning competences for staff;
  - Quality assurance framework for e-courses.
- Established e-learning centres with trained staff and specific business strategy;
- Training material for teachers regarding e-learning and ICT for lifelong learning;
- Pilot projects (implemented e-courses).

D-TRANSFORM

DigiTal Resources As a New Strategical Factor for a Renovation of Modernization in higher education

Website: http://www.dtransform.eu/

Runtime: 01 Sep 2014 – 31 Aug 2017

Supported / co-funded by: Erasmus+

Partners: Fondation Maison Des Sciences De L'Homme, FR (coordinator); Université de Lorraine, FR; Sero Consulting Ltd, UK; Fundacio per a la Universitat Oberta de Catalunya, ES; Politecnico di Milano – METID, IT; European Distance and E-Learning Network, UK; Budapest University of Technology and Economics, HU.

Project representative to be contacted for further info: Angela Procoli (procoli@msh-paris.fr)

The D-TRANSFORM project is a first attempt to set up a "University Leader Program" at the European level, addressed to university presidents and vice-presidents on the role of e-Education in shaping University strategies. It gathers together specialists of e-Education from various institutions (University, higher education ministries, consultancy in learning innovation, e-Education networks) and primarily considers that digital technologies, like Massive Open Online Courses, (MOOCs) and Open Educational Resources are an essential lever for transforming the higher education systems and adapting them to the new needs of youth and requirements of work-market (lifelong training).

D-TRANSFORM produced recommendations on various aspects of a university strategy on the use of digital tools. Based on these recommendations, D-TRANSFORM have set up two leadership schools, dedicated, for the 1st time in Europe, to the university governances.

Main target groups of the project: HE Institutions and schools, presidents, vice-presidents and staff involved in management at the highest level

Significant public results:

Guidelines of a training program for university leaders on the base of state-of-the art and context analysis of European and national public policies, a business model for online training, rationalising the costs of HE through the use of digital teaching by evidence-based analysis and case studies:

- Public Digital Policies in Higher Education – A comparative survey between Spain, France, Italy and the United Kingdom.
- Business models for opening up education – Sustainability of MOOCs, OER and related online education approaches in higher education in Europe.
- Open Educational Resource, a lever for digital transition of higher education?
- Guidelines for governance of HE institutions.

Organisation of **two leadership schools** for university leaders (presidents and vice-presidents) of partner universities in 2016 and 2017.

MOOC on Digital resources as catalyst for change in University

EduTeach

Continuing Education to Preschool Teachers and Educational Directors through Online Trainings

Website: http://www.eduteach.odl.org/

Runtime: 01 Sep 2015 - 01 Sep 2018

Supported / co-funded by: Erasmus+

Partners: Institute for Innovation in Learning, University of Erlangen Nuremberg, DE (coordinator); City of Tampere, Early childhood and basic education, FI; StePS srl – Strategies & Tools to Enhance People's Skills, IT; Militos Consulting S.A., EL; Innovation Training Center, S.L., ES; Confederación de Centros de Educación Infantil, ES; Budapest University of Technology and Economics, HU; Akademie für Kindergarten, Kita und Hort Brode und Hovermann OHG, DE; Università degli Studi di Macerata, IT; Inštitut za simbolno analizo in razvoj informacijskih tehnologij velenje zavod, SI.

Project representative to be contacted for further info: Michael Zwanziger (Michael.Zwanziger@ili.fau.de)

The EduTeach project designs, tests and implements a modular training program adapted to the needs and interests of those responsible in education and care for young children (0-6 years) across Europe. To allow both flexible and individual learning, the training offers are based on ICT (Ilias) and incorporate a fair balance between interactive and self-study learning activities. Using results from a user needs analysis and evaluations of the implementation of trainings, EduTeach further tends to forward research and development on models, methods, and didactic strategies for effective online training to educators, preschool teachers and education directors.

Main target groups of the project: preschool teachers, educational directors

Significant public results:

Joint Scientific Research – **User Needs Analysis** and Methodology Development (2016) – public report

Tutoring Guidelines (2016): teaching approaches, supporting strategies, tutor's profile and competencies and tools that can be used for both synchronous and asynchronous communication/interaction

Set of Educational Materials - Curriculum and Training Content: 10 modules in Early Childhood Education and Care related topics that the learning needs analyses proved needed. Default courses in English, learning materials are translated (at least 4/Hungarian, Slovenian, Greek, German, Spanish) based on country-specific analyses.

At present (May 2017) two modules are already freely available to study:

- Oktatásmódszertan és játék a személyek közötti konfliktusok kezelésére (Hungarian);
- Was ist schon normal? Kompaktkurs Verhaltensauffälligkeiten bei Kindern (German).

VOCAL

Vocational Online Collaboration for Active Learning

Website: http://www.vocalerasmus.eu/

Runtime: 01 Nov 2016 - 31 Oct 2018

Supported / co-funded by: Erasmus+

Partners: Budapest University of Technology and Economics, HU (coordinator); Baden-Würtemberg Cooperative State University Heilbronn, DE; Universidad de la Iglesia de Deusto, ES; Vytautas Magnus University, LT; Lithuanian Association of Distance and e-Learning, LT; Ogres Tehnikums, LV.

Project representative to be contacted for further info: Denes Zarka (zarkakis@edu-inno.bme.hu)

The project fosters open collaboration of HE teachers and VET trainers to design online, open and collaborative learning activities for diverse target groups embedding digital, social, and intercultural competences. In order to meet this aim, the partnership develops training materials and organise face-to-face, weeklong training events where teachers and trainers will be able to

- develop skills to digitalise quality learning resources, to design online collaborative learning activities embedding digital, social, and intercultural competence development, and to tutor international, intercultural diverse learner groups;
- collaborate designing mutually online and open curriculum for diverse international learner groups, and
- establish open educational practices for future references.

Main target groups of the project: HE teachers, VET trainers

Significant public results:

Training materials are available through VOCAL Moodle platform with content freely available to download. The material is tested in joint staff training events by 24 educators from the partner institutions:

- Training material on digitalization of quality learning resources;
- Training material on designing online collaborative learning activities;
- Training material on tutoring diverse learner groups.

Testimonies of Open Educational Practices from HE teachers and VET trainers

6 re-developed courses, result of the collaborative learning and working process of delegated staff members (public availability to be defined)